P9-DBI-485

Architecture

Titles in the World History Series

The Age of Feudalism
Ancient Greece
The Ancient Near East
Architecture
Aztec Civilization
The Cuban Revolution
The Early Middle Ages
Egypt of the Pharaohs
Elizabethan England
The End of the Cold War
The Enlightenment
The French and Indian War
The French Revolution
Greek and Roman Theater
Hitler's Reich
The Hundred Years' War
The Inquisition
Modern Japan
The Relocation of the North American Indians
The Roman Empire
The Roman Republic
The Russian Revolution
Traditional Japan
The Travels of Marco Polo
Women's Suffrage

Architecture

by
Paula Bryant Pratt

720.9
PRA

Lucent Books, P.O. Box 289011, San Diego, CA 92198-9011

Library of Congress Cataloging-in-Publication Data

Pratt, Paula, 1959-
    Architecture / by Paula Bryant Pratt.
        p. cm.—(World history series)
    Includes bibliographical references (p.) and index.
    ISBN 1-56006-286-X (alk. paper)
    1. Architecture—Juvenile literature. [1. Architecture.]
I.Title. II. Series.
NA2555.P73   1995
720'.9—dc20   94-23499
                                       CIP
                                       AC

DF HB EX S D

Copyright 1995 by Lucent Books, Inc., P.O. Box 289011,
San Diego, California 92198-9011

Printed in the U.S.A.

No part of this book may be reproduced or used in any other
form or by any other means, electrical, mechanical, or otherwise, including, but not limited to, photocopy, recording, or
any information storage and retrieval system, without prior
written permission from the publisher.

Contents

Foreword

Each year on the first day of school, nearly every history teacher faces the task of explaining why his or her students should study history. One logical answer to this question is that exploring what happened in our past explains how the things we often take for granted—our customs, ideas, and institutions—came to be. As statesman and historian Winston Churchill put it, "Every nation or group of nations has its own tale to tell. Knowledge of the trials and struggles is necessary to all who would comprehend the problems, perils, challenges, and opportunities which confront us today." Thus, a study of history puts modern ideas and institutions in perspective. For example, though the founders of the United States were talented and creative thinkers, they clearly did not invent the concept of democracy. Instead, they adapted some democratic ideas that had originated in ancient Greece and with which the Romans, the British, and others had experimented. An exploration of these cultures, then, reveals their very real connection to us through institutions that continue to shape our daily lives.

Another reason often given for studying history is the idea that lessons exist in the past from which contemporary societies can benefit and learn. This idea, although controversial, has always been an intriguing one for historians. Those who agree that society can benefit from the past often quote philosopher George Santayana's famous statement, "Those who cannot remember the past are condemned to repeat it." Historians who ascribe to Santayana's philosophy believe that, for example, studying the events that led up to the major world wars or other significant historical events would allow society to chart a different and more favorable course in the future.

Just as difficult as convincing students to realize the importance of studying history is the search for useful and interesting supplementary materials that present historical events in a context that can be easily understood. The volumes in Lucent Books' World History Series attempt to present a broad, balanced, and penetrating view of the march of history. Ancient Egypt's important wars and rulers, for example, are presented against the rich and colorful backdrop of Egyptian religious, social, and cultural developments. The series engages the reader by enhancing historical events with these cultural contexts. For example, in *Ancient Greece*, the text covers the role of women in that society. Slavery is discussed in *The Roman Empire*, as well as how slaves earned their freedom. The numerous and varied aspects of everyday life in these and other societies are explored in each volume of the series. Additionally, the series covers the major political, cultural, and philosophical ideas as the torch of civilization is passed from ancient Mesopotamia and Egypt, through Greece, Rome, Medieval Europe, and other world cultures, to the modern day.

The material in the series is formatted in a thorough, precise, and organized manner. Each volume offers the reader a comprehensive and clearly written overview of an important historical event or period. The topic under discussion is placed in a broad historical context. For example, *The Italian Renaissance* begins with a discussion of the High Middle Ages and the loss of central control that allowed certain Italian cities to develop artistically. The book ends by looking forward to the Reformation and interpreting the societal changes that grew out of the Renaissance. Thus, students are not only involved in an historical era, but also enveloped by the events leading up to that era and the events following it.

One important and unique feature in the World History Series is the primary and secondary source quotations that richly supplement each volume. These quotes are useful in a number of ways. First, they allow students access to sources they would not normally be exposed to because of the difficulty and obscurity of the original source. The quotations range from interesting anecdotes to far-sighted cultural perspectives and are drawn from historical witnesses both past and present. Second, the quotes demonstrate how and where historians themselves derive their information on the past as they strive to reach a consensus on historical events. Lastly, all of the quotes are footnoted, familiarizing students with the citation process and allowing them to verify quotes and/or look up the original source if the quote piques their interest.

Finally, the books in the World History Series provide a detailed launching point for further research. Each book contains a bibliography specifically geared toward student research. A second, annotated bibliography introduces students to all the sources the author consulted when compiling the book. A chronology of important dates gives students an overview, at a glance, of the topic covered. Where applicable, a glossary of terms is included.

In short, the series is designed not only to acquaint readers with the basics of history, but also to make them aware that their lives are a part of an ongoing human saga. Perhaps they will then come to the same realization as famed historian Arnold Toynbee. In his monumental work, *A Study of History*, he wrote about becoming aware of history flowing through him in a mighty current, and of his own life "welling like a wave in the flow of this vast tide."

Important Dates in the History of Architecture

2570 B.C.	A.D. 100	200	300	400	500	600	700	800	900

2570 B.C.
Great Pyramid of Khufu at Giza, Egypt, is completed

1290 B.C.
Temple of Amun at Karnak, Egypt, is completed

447–438 B.C.
The Parthenon, Athens

A.D. 118–128
The Pantheon, Rome

300–400
Old St. Peter's, Rome

532–537
Church of the Hagia Sophia, Istanbul, Turkey

1063
Cathedral of Pisa, Italy, is begun

1194–1260
Chartres cathedral, France

1200–1300
The Alhambra, Granada, Spain

1418
Cathedral of Santa Maria del Fiore, Florence, is completed

1502
The Tempietto, Rome

1506
Reconstruction of St. Peter's is begun

17th century
The Taj Mahal, Agra, India

1645–1652
Cornaro Chapel, Rome

1658–1670
Church of Sant'Andrea al Quirinale, Rome

1675–1709
Reconstruction of St. Paul's Cathedral, London

1732–1762
The Fountain of Trevi, Rome

mid–1700s
Bath Circus and Royal Crescent, Bath, England

1748
Strawberry Hill, England, is begun

1785-1798
Virginia State Capitol, Richmond

1795–1807
Fonthill Abbey, England

1000	1100	1200	1300	1400	1500	1600	1700	1800	1900	1983

1809
University of Virginia campus is begun

1812–1817
Regent's Park in London is designed

1851
Crystal Palace, London

1867–1883
Brooklyn Bridge, New York

1875–1886
Statue of Liberty, New York

1887–1889
Eiffel Tower, Paris

1909
Robie House, Chicago

1913
Woolworth Building, New York

1910
Casa Mila apartment building, Barcelona, Spain

1925–1926
The Bauhaus, Dessau, Germany

1930
Chrysler Building in New York is completed

1931
Empire State Building, New York

1931–1940
Rockefeller Center, New York

1954–1958
Seagram Building, New York

1955
Chapel of Notre Dame du Haut, Ronchamp, France

1962
Chestnut Hill House, Philadelphia

1956–1959
Guggenheim Museum, New York

1965–1974
Kresge College campus, Santa Cruz, California

1975–1980
Piazza d'Italia, New Orleans

1977
Centre Pompidou, Paris

1980–1983
Portland Public Service Building, Oregon

The Impulse to Build

The impulse to build, to make a mark on one's surroundings, has always been part of human nature. Although architecture encompasses all the structures people build and use, in its history there are public buildings, palaces, monuments, and other structures that reflect a grand architectural impulse, the impulse to construct something magnificent and memorable, a testimony to the ingenuity of both architect and civilization.

Architecture of timeless greatness, structures that stir cultures beyond the ones that produced them, creatively combine beauty of form with fulfillment of function, or purpose. (Form is what a building looks like; function is what a building is used for.) An architect should take into account both a building's appearance and the reason for building it.

Form and Function

Architects consider buildings beautiful if they are designed with four principles in mind. First, the building's elements must balance each other. Second, the structure should incorporate rhythm, or regular pattern. For example, the way windows are set in a wall can present a rhythmic pattern. Third, the parts of the building must be sized in proportion to one another. Fourth, the building must be harmonious in its scale—the relative size of the building and its parts in relation to the surroundings.

These elements of form—balance, rhythm, proportion, and scale—can be emphasized by the architect in a variety of ways. For example, a temple that is intended to inspire awe and a public building meant to appear open and inviting will differ greatly in form.

A functional building fits its purpose. Most functional buildings are durable enough to provide shelter and protection from the elements. They are also carefully designed to be comfortable for the people who use them and to efficiently serve the needs of their users.

A truly great work of architecture cannot be merely decorative. If it lacks functional elements such as strength and efficiency, it will not stand the test of time. But a great work of architecture cannot be merely functional, either. Without a pleasing form, a building is soulless, little more than a shell, and does nothing to celebrate the culture in which it was built.

A truly great building—one that appeals to many cultures and whose appeal lasts beyond its own time—is one whose design pleasingly meshes form and function in an ingenious, striking combination. Often in such masterpieces the practical elements transcend their useful purpose and add to a structure's beauty. For example, the flying buttresses, or stone arches, that brace the outer walls of a medieval cathedral are one of the most beautiful aspects of the cathedral's design, yet they are also one of the most practical elements, since they keep the church from collapsing. In great architecture, then, form and function unite.

Great works of architecture share the qualities of functionality and beauty of form. But the cultures that produce them vary widely, as do the structures themselves. Two outstanding architectural works of different eras, the Church of the Hagia Sophia in Istanbul, Turkey, and Rockefeller Center in New York City, demonstrate how great architecture can transcend culture. Each project has its own merits; each beautifully fulfills its purpose in its own way; and each cuts across time in its appeal.

Hagia Sophia

The Church of the Hagia Sophia, built during the Byzantine Empire in the sixth century, was designed to glorify both God and the empire. Because worshipers were to gather inside the building, not outside it, most of the decoration is lavished on the interior. A visitor entering the church is transported with awe at the overwhelming size and intricacy of the inside of the church, which is dominated by a huge central dome. The architects planned a

The interior of Hagia Sophia, built in the sixth century, is richly decorated with intricate designs.

mysterious, glittering effect when they pierced the dome's base with a ring of windows. The light they admit causes the interior's richly carved marble walls to shimmer. The combination of massive size and exquisite ornament produces a breathtaking effect, thus effectively fulfilling the purpose of Emperor Justinian in designing it—to celebrate the grandeur of his religion and his empire. The Byzantine Empire itself is long gone, but the beauty of the Church of the Hagia Sophia has never dimmed.

Rockefeller Center

A modern-day example of an innovative blend of form and function is New York's Rockefeller Center, an inviting complex of shops, theaters, and courtyards within a cluster of tall office towers. Conceived with the idea of honoring growth and progress in human history, the area was also meant to be a place where people could seek refuge from the busy city. An enormous bronze statue hovering over a marble fountain overlooks an outdoor café and an ice-skating rink. All combine to create a gracious, attractive setting, where visitors can unwind. Rockefeller Center is unique in that it provides open space in the midst of a crowded city, space dedicated not merely to commerce, but to human enjoyment. Built in the 1930s, its appeal endures today; its fitness of purpose and its beauty are confirmed by the people who make enthusiastic use of the refreshing, upbeat atmosphere it was designed to provide.

Rockefeller Center provides an excellent example of urban architecture designed to provide city inhabitants with a relaxing, enjoyable break from the bustle of downtown.

While radically different from each other, both the Church of the Hagia Sophia and Rockefeller Center make imaginative, innovative use of form and function to present to the world a work of lasting beauty and worth. Throughout history, this goal has been the dream of every great architect.

1 The Ancient World

The architecture of the Egyptians, Greeks, and Romans is remarkable for its breakthroughs. For example, in addition to their impressive pyramids, ancient Egyptian architects built the first great post-and-beam structures in stone. Furthermore, Egypt's temples were the first to use columns decoratively, not just as pillars to hold up a roof. In turn, the Greeks developed the idea of decorative columns and perfected post-and-beam construction. Roman architects borrowed ideas from the Greeks and added their own magnificent variations using arches, domes, and vaults. These early achievements have left their mark on architecture throughout history.

Egyptian Architecture

Ancient Egyptian architecture made revolutionary strides. The early Egyptians began over five thousand years ago, by constructing shelters from reed stalks or palm fronds; they ended by erecting towering monuments of laboriously quarried stone. The early structures were primitive but versatile, as writers Helen and Richard Leacroft point out:

> Early buildings were made from reeds or palm fronds, matted together and strengthened with reeds tied in bundles and fastened at the corners and across the tops of the walls. The heads of the vertical reeds, left free above the walls, provided a crowning decoration. . . . Reeds tied in bundles could also be used as columns . . . and these and the walls when plastered with mud became quite strong, but they did not have a long life.[1]

The cliffs rimming the Nile Valley offered building materials ranging from soft sandstone to dense granite. The riverbanks themselves supplied clay for brick. The challenge to early Egyptians was how to quarry the stone, or carry it from the cliffs to the building sites, where the increasingly grand structures they planned would be erected. According to Helen and Richard Leacroft, hauling raw materials became an ordeal as the Egyptians' projects got bigger:

> The Ancient Egyptians had to move all their building materials by manpower because they had no cranes or mechanical equipment. At first this was not serious because they used small stones, but when they increased the size of their buildings they used huge blocks weighing many tons.[2]

An illustration depicts Egyptian slaves quarrying and transporting the huge stone blocks necessary for erecting the pyramids. These ancient monuments continue to awe and astound millions of visitors each year.

Just how they did it remains a mystery, but a popular theory maintains that the heavy stones were dragged on wooden ramps, drawn by oxen or by the workers themselves. If the stones had to be brought in from far away, they probably were ferried down the Nile River on rafts.

The heavy, static appearance of ancient Egypt's architecture gives it the reputation for being unimaginative. Marvin Trachtenberg and Isabelle Hyman disagree:

> Egyptian architecture is generally regarded as manifesting little change. But this is a modern viewpoint, seen through eyes grown accustomed to overnight developments. A more appropriate perspective sets Egypt against the Neolithic age from which it emerged and in which it took early man thousands of years to achieve the most rudimentary post-and-lintel dolmens. . . . From this viewpoint the emergence of Egyptian pyramids in [a] few generations . . . seems a breakthrough of spellbinding potency

[power] and speed. The later development of the temple is similarly astonishing in its creative energy and attainment.[3]

Both the pyramid and the temple, then, were original and visionary building types.

The Pyramids

Egypt's pyramids, huge monuments constructed of stacked stone blocks, housed hidden chambers, or rooms. The innermost chamber was a tomb intended to hold the body of the ruler, the pharaoh. The pyramid itself was a fortress meant to protect the body and the treasures buried with it from robbers. It was also meant to symbolize the Egyptians' belief that their rulers would ultimately conquer death and rise again, immortal.

Why the four-sided, pointed form? Perhaps it best demonstrated, through mass and balance, the Egyptians' respect for permanence. A pyramid is stable, grounded on earth, yet pointing heavenward. Its great size is a suitable reminder of the pharaoh's presumed power to reach through death into everlasting life. And, quite simply, a pyramid's stark, clean outline is beautiful, as Victoria Kloss Ball comments: "In the . . . pyramidal style the aesthetic appeal rests with the silhouette of . . . [the] triangle against the sky."[4]

The timeless appeal of these imposing and mysterious structures is due to their elegant design and the sheer impact of their size. That the Egyptians could have dragged, hoisted, and stacked these weighty stones with such precision is miraculous. The clean, solid lines of the pyramid reflect its double purpose—to protect the hidden contents and to strike awe in viewers. The pyramid shape serves to guard secrets while boldly pointing to them.

Egypt's most famous pyramid is the tomb of Khufu, or Cheops, at Giza. Called the Great Pyramid, it was completed around 2570 B.C. No Egyptian pyramid erected before or after it came close in size, as Trachtenberg and Hyman point out:

> Khufu's pyramid at Giza . . . is rightly called the Great Pyramid for its advanced technology as well as for its size, unmatched by its predecessors or by the smaller (though still enormous) pyramids alongside it that were built by Khufu's successors. . . . The Great Pyramid is so immense—originally 482 feet high on a plan 760 feet square (even St. Peter's in Rome or London's Houses of Parliament would fit inside it!)—that the quarrying and lifting of its blocks, like all megalithic construction, have continued to puzzle archaeologists.[5]

The silent majesty of Khufu's pyramid hides a secret—as with other, smaller

The Great Pyramid that houses the tomb of Khufu is filled with intricate passageways and secret chambers.

pyramids, hidden passageways thread through the inner core of the structure. The sloping outer wall contains two entrances, one higher than the other. The original, higher, entrance is accessible through a hinged stone acting as a door. From that hidden doorway, a steep tunnel, only four feet high and less than three and a half feet wide, plunges at a twenty-degree slant into the pyramid's center. A lower entrance was forced into the pyramid's face by a young Arab scholar named al-Ma'mūn, who was seeking ancient astronomical maps rumored to be hidden within. This forced entrance is now the only way into the tomb of Khufu: The original entrance is sealed.

The cramped passageways of the Great Pyramid of Khufu lead to rewards for those daring enough to enter. A chamber with a pointed roof, called the Queen's Chamber, lies at the end of one of the branching passages. The 18-foot-square chamber is bare, probably unfinished. From the Queen's Chamber tilts an astonishing, 28-foot-high passageway called the Grand Gallery, made of tiers of stone, narrowing as they ascend. This passageway, built without mortar, stretches for 157 feet and leads to the King's Chamber, a large walled room roofed in pink granite. The treasures it once contained, including Khufu's body, are gone. But the ingenious structure of the Great Pyramid's inner passageways and chambers, as well as the massive size and simple beauty of its exterior, continues to inspire awe in observers.

The Great Pyramid is an example of a primitive building method—megalith construction, stacking of stones one on top of the other—taken to a brilliant extreme. More advanced, but less immediately recognizable as Egyptian than the trademark pyramid, however, is the temple. In its temples, the ancient Egyptians developed two elements, post-and-beam construction and the decorative column. These two innovations influenced the Greek and Roman architects who followed.

The Egyptian Temple

The earliest Egyptians had already learned to form supporting columns from reeds and to stretch horizontal beams across them to form a roof. To achieve the same construction in stone, architects had to develop the post-and-beam system, in which many columns are set close together, to ensure that their roofs would hold up. In the hands of the Egyptians, this need for many columns was transformed into the source of an art form. In fact the column became a way for Egypt to honor its past visually, since architects began designing stone columns that mimicked the curved fronds, buds, and petals of their culture's earliest columns of reed and papyrus plants. Helen and Richard Leacroft describe the effect: "The stone columns were carved to resemble the bundles of papyrus stems, with their flowers forming a decorative head or capital; or the palm tree with its fronds or the lotus buds tied round the posts."[6]

Elegant column forms were showcased in the Egyptian temples, which were popular between 1580 and 1085 B.C. These immense buildings relied on row upon row of decorated pillars to support their vast interiors. The elaborate temple plan was usually made up of four sections: the pylon, the peristyle court, the hypostyle (many-columned) hall, and the chambered sanctuary. Each section was more

The Temple of Amun at Karnak shows the repetition of many columns so popular with the Egyptians. Most Egyptians were not allowed much beyond these columns.

hidden than the last. Common worshipers were not allowed to venture past the hypostyle hall. Only the ruler and his priests could penetrate into the inner chambers.

Visitors approached the temple pylon, or gate, along a wide avenue lined with statues. This pylon, a massive stone structure, was adorned with flags and painted carvings of the pharaoh and various gods. It opened onto the peristyle courtyard, an area surrounded by a single row of columns. Central doors led to the hypostyle hall, whose size required the support of a forest of pillars. Beyond this hall lay the enclosed chambers where the god to whom the temple was dedicated was said to live.

The temple reflected the Egyptian architects' purpose of inspiring religious awe. The shift from open to enclosed space created a progression from sunlight to shadow. While the peristyle court was relatively exposed to the light, the shad-

owy hypostyle hall received light only from a gap near the roof called a clerestory (clear story). Beams resting on top of columns elevated the room's ceiling enough to let in shafts of sunlight. (This technique, originating with the Egyptians, was used with flair centuries later in medieval cathedral architecture.) Visitors privileged to continue into the deeper recesses of the walled chambers were plunged into murky gloom. This movement from light to darkness conveyed a sense of mystery, reminding the people of the power of their ruler, the temple god, and its priests.

The Egyptians found beauty in the stately repetition of the temple's basic elements. Ball comments that our modern eyes see a "forest of masonry rather than a field of space . . . [but] to the Egyptian interested in time and eternity rather than in space and extension this may not have been undesirable."[7]

A Hypnotic Temple

According to Architecture: From Pre-History to Post-Modernism, *the Temple of Amun at Karnak is a stunning example of an Egyptian temple, an architectural form developed by the ancient culture that introduced the pyramid. The authors, art historians Marvin Trachtenberg and Isabelle Hyman, describe the hypnotic effect of its interior detail.*

"The compounding and elaboration of the basic components of the Karnak temple program must have produced a profound effect on the worshiper. Even today, the beholder is overwhelmed by the scale and richness, staggered by the repetitions, and transported by the architectural fantasies of the priesthood. One aspect in particular was stunningly visionary: the Hypostyle Hall of Seti I and his son Ramasses II. This largest of all hypostyle halls measured 340 feet in width and 170 feet in depth; its roof of stone slabs was supported by 134 columns standing in 16 rows—7 rows on each side formed of columns 9 feet thick and 42 feet high, framing 2 rows of larger columns almost 12 feet in diameter and 69 feet in height that ran through three central processional aisles. The columns and walls were everywhere incised with polychromed [colored] figures and hieroglyphs in relief, intensifying the presence of the columnar masses in the narrow interspaces. The columns were of two types: closed papyrus buds on the sides, and open papyrus flowers in the two great center rows. While the roof that the papyrus-bud columns support was closed— the later aisles having no lighting of their own—the roof of the three central aisles rose above that of the sides, leaving a vertical gap called a clerestory, which contained slitlike windows. This early clerestory allowed considerable light to fall mainly into the three aisles, fading off into the side aisles. The effect was that the closed-bud columns of the side aisles appeared to lift forward the light in the central aisles and blossom into the papyrus flowers. The success of this feat of architectural illusionism—achieving the sense of organic growth in columns nearly 12 feet in diameter—was augmented by obscuring the block connecting the papyrus flowers with the clerestory ceiling, so that the flowers appeared to rise unencumbered toward the light."

In the sheer size and bulk of both temple and pyramid, the Egyptians expressed their culture's unique situation. They seemed to want to confront the sweeping emptiness of their desert surroundings with creations of weight and substance. Their architecture provided them with an anchor to both present and future. According to Trachtenberg and Hyman, the breathtaking natural beauty of their surroundings "posed a compelling challenge: to create an architecture that would match the scale and grandeur of the river, the mountains, and the desert."[8]

Greek Architecture

Egyptian culture was still very much alive when Greek civilization began its rise around 1100 B.C. Ancient Greece came into full creative flower between the eighth and sixth centuries B.C. During the cultural high point, between the winding down of the Persian Wars (479 B.C.) and

the beginning of the Peloponnesian War (431 B.C.), Greece's crowning architectural achievement, the Parthenon, was conceived and built.

Temples like the Parthenon were Greece's most important architectural form. Unlike the religious buildings of many other Western cultures, they were not designed to accommodate gatherings of worshipers. A Greek temple's only occupant was a statue of the deity to whom the building was dedicated. The temple sheltered the statue and was the symbolic home of the god or goddess. The simplest temples consisted of a single room, or cella, with a porch in front. Often, a second porch was added at the back for balance. More expensive temples featured a ring of columns around the cella and porches to make the building look similar from all sides. Some temples in wealthy areas added a second row of columns around the first.

Since Greek temples used post-and-beam construction, large open interiors were not possible—an extensive roof

This view of the market at Athens reveals several temples built to honor Greek gods. Unlike temples in other cultures, Greek temples were not built as places of worship.

Architecture Expresses Culture

In his classic book The Ascent of Man, *scholar Jacob Bronowski explains that for ancient culture, architecture was a process of discovery similar to science today.*

"[H]uman achievement . . . is not a museum of finished constructions. It is a progress. . . . The stonework of Machu Picchu in the Andes and the geometry of the Alhambra in Moorish Spain seem to us, five centuries later, exquisite works of decorative art. But if we stop there, we miss the originality of the two cultures that made them. Within their time, they are constructions as arresting and important for their peoples as the architecture of DNA for us."

would have had to be supported frequently inside, and the numerous columns would give a sense of clutter, instead of an airy, spacious feel. But the Greeks did not need large temples because most of their ceremonies took place outdoors. The faithful made offerings at altars placed outside the temples. As Ball puts it, "Greek architecture was an architecture for exterior viewing. It was an architecture of the inner cloister and the open court."[9]

Both the Greeks and the Egyptians worked in stone, using the only structural system they had perfected—post-and-beam. Faced with the method's limitations, the two societies made very different choices, which reveal their attitudes about life. The Egyptians wanted their temples to be both impressive and mysterious: Enormity required the crowding of numerous interior columns; secret rituals had to be hidden, performed in inner recesses obscured by thick walls. By contrast, a Greek temple's columns did not form a barrier. On the contrary, as

writer Susan Woodford points out, the interior was in plain view: "The statue of the divinity looking out of the door at the east end of the temple would be well situated to watch the ceremonies. The worshippers standing around the altar would have a good chance to admire the temple."[10] This arrangement invited a feeling of connection between the god or goddess and the people, and demonstrated to the public that the temple belonged to them.

Union between people and architecture was important to the Greeks, and they carried this connection into their temple designs. Each part of a temple had special details that made it a complete entity; yet all the structure's different parts worked together perfectly to make up a graceful and unified whole. Because of its interwoven patterns, Greek architecture has often been called frozen music.

Greek Columns

The care Greek architects lavished on the simple column shows their devotion to de-

Greeks lavished detail on their stone columns, a heavily used design element. Two types of columns are shown here: Ionic, with flat, cushion-like capitals (left) and Corinthian, which featured acanthus leaves.

tail. There were two main column styles, Doric and Ionic. Both types were in use by the fifth century B.C. The sturdy Doric column was four to six times taller than it measured around. Ionic columns were thinner, eight to ten times higher than the diameter. Columns of both types caught light and shadow with deep vertical grooves called flutes, and both types were slightly tapered. Their shape and texture made them almost come alive, as if they were muscled limbs flexing under the weight of the structure.

A significant difference between Ionic and Doric columns was the shape of the capital, or top. Doric capitals looked like flattened cushions, and Ionic capitals looked like inward-curling scrolls or shells. A variation on the Ionic column, called the Corinthian, appeared in the late fifth century B.C. Corinthian capitals resembled clusters of acanthus leaves curling outward. (Acanthus is a common Mediterranean herb.) As with the Egyptians, the Greeks made their columns elegant as well as practical, but in Greek architecture the

style of column decoration was related to the overall style of the building. This style was called an order. The Parthenon, for example, was a temple of the Doric order.

The Parthenon

Designed by architects Ictinis and Callicrates and built between 477 and 432 B.C., the Parthenon has a dramatic history. In 490 the Greeks had won a crucial battle at Marathon that kept an invading Persian army from sweeping across the Mediterranean. In triumph and relief, the Greeks decided to memorialize their victory by replacing an older stone temple with a new one in marble. It would be dedicated to the goddess Athena, who they believed protected the city of Athens.

The temple site was the Acropolis, meaning "city on the height." This striking location, sheer cliff on all sides but the west, was the city's religious and cultural center. Construction for the beautiful new temple was well under way when the Persians suddenly invaded Athens in 480 B.C.

(Left) This view of the Acropolis in Athens shows why it was aptly named "the city on the height." Athens was destroyed during an invasion by the Persians in 480 B.C. When Pericles commissioned the reconstruction of the Acropolis in 450 B.C., he lavished special attention on the Parthenon. (Below) The interior of the Parthenon, with the huge gold and ivory statue of Athena.

They destroyed the entire city, paying special attention to the buildings at the Acropolis. Only rubble remained.

The furious Athenians vowed to leave the Acropolis in ruins as a dramatically visible war memorial. However, by 450 B.C., an ambitious and optimistic new leader, Pericles, was in power, and Greece felt strong again. Pericles decided to use the people's defense fund to finance a complete reconstruction of the Acropolis, hiring the greatest sculptors, architects, and builders. Pericles lavished special bounty on the Parthenon, the temple that would house a colossal sculpture of Athena.

The Parthenon is unique in many ways, one of which is its unusual size. It had to be big to hold the forty-foot gold and ivory statue of Athena created by the famous sculptor Phidias. To reinforce the long roof, a U-shaped procession of slender columns surrounded the goddess figure within. The columns could be slim because they were double-tiered, or stacked two layers high, one on top of the other. The outer columns were single Doric-style columns, thirty-four feet tall.

Eight columns each, instead of the usual six, lined each end of the building. Seventeen columns faced each side, following the convention of having the number of side columns equal twice the number of columns on each end, plus one.

In the case of the Parthenon, however, the entire structure's appearance grew from number relationships. The architects chose their temple's measurements with a plan in mind. For example, the temple's length is a little over twice its width in a ratio of 9:4. Its ends have a width-to-height ratio of 9:4 as well. And the distance between each column (from center to center) is a little more than twice the diameter of each column, again a ratio of 9:4. Woodford comments on this precise plan's beauty: "The whole building, though built in a simple way out of simple parts, has a coherence and harmony that is rooted in mathematics."[11]

The Parthenon's most sophisticated feature is found in the subtle adjustments designed to make the temple look graceful and balanced to the human eye. By constructing it without a single truly straight line or perfectly right angle, the architects compensated for the eye's tendency to distort what it sees. The Parthenon's base and roof are slightly arched, higher in the middle than at the sides. The building's sides curve subtly inward. The columns bulge just a bit near the middle, to prevent their tops from seeming too narrow. And no column is straight: each one tilts inward, to allow the eye to see them all as upright. Without these built-in imperfections, called optical refinements, the Parthenon could have seemed predictable and stiff. Instead, it had a vital energy, a gentle eccentricity despite its grandeur. This quality probably seemed human and welcoming to the people who erected it as a monument to honor the deity who watched over their city.

The Parthenon as it would have looked during the days of Pericles. The architect of the Parthenon constructed it without a single true line or perfectly straight angle to compensate for the human eye's distortion.

Roman Architecture

The Roman Empire began its takeover of the Mediterranean region after 700 B.C. Romans were fanatical builders. Erecting their own structures in a conquered city symbolized control. Often their civilization is remembered as having copied architectural styles, such as column orders, from the Greeks. But the ancient Romans were phenomenal engineers, and they achieved at least two architectural breakthroughs: mastery of both arcuated (arched) and concrete block construction. Ball praises Roman architects' contributions: "The Romans were architectural borrowers of architectural dressing from Greece, of structure from the east . . . [however,] they were imaginative and daring developers of classical form and great engineers."[12]

The Arch

While the Romans did not invent the arch, which had already been used occasionally by the Egyptians, they exploited the full possibilities of the device. Ancient Rome's enthusiasm for arch, vault, and dome has been called a structural revolution, because arches solved many of the problems presented by the simpler, more limited post-and-beam system. In architecture, an arch is a curve made from wedge-shaped blocks. A building supported by arches can weigh more than one held up by beams because arches get stronger when pushed downward. This happens because compression, or downward force, locks the wedges in place. In addition to shouldering loads, arches with proper support can bridge wide areas, making them ideal for spanning large interior spaces. Unlike Greek or Egyptian temples that used post-and-beam construction, Roman buildings did not need forests of pillars on the inside. Thus, thanks to arcuated construction, Roman architects could play with the impact of open interior spaces to an extent that had not been achieved by the Greeks and the Egyptians.

In fact, the Romans discovered a special arch called a groin vault, a variation on an earlier form, the barrel vault. A barrel, or tunnel, vault was an arch that extended lengthwise and became a semicircular, tunnel-like roof. The trouble with barrel vaults was that they needed continuous support. They also made the rooms they covered hard to light, since their only openings were far apart, at either end. The new groin vault was simply two barrel vaults that crossed at right angles. Their intersection formed a square that could be strengthened from below. These cross-shaped vaults could be combined into larger patterns. Since a groin vault had four openings, one at each end of the cross, while barrel vaults had only two, groin-vaulted roofs let in more light from different angles.

Trachtenberg and Hyman stress the lasting significance of ancient Rome's development of the arch:

> The arch was one of mankind's great discoveries. It enabled architects to span gaps with economy and strength and to enclose vast interiors with assurance. The arch was to architecture what the wheel was to transportation and industry. . . . Today, it would be difficult for a builder to find a mason anywhere in the Western world capable of building a sizable masonry arch. The art of arch building, developed

The Romans' development of the arch, here clearly seen in this picture of the ancient Colosseum, was one of the most important contributions to architecture.

and practiced for over two thousand years, has been all but lost. But for centuries, the highest technical skills of the architectural craft were devoted to erecting arches and vaults.[13]

Rome's second major innovation was its discovery of a new building material—concrete. Cement, made of lime, sand, and water, had been known to builders from the fourth century B.C. The ancient Romans combined this material with a local volcanic ash called pozzolana, which dried to tremendous strength. Poured concrete hardened into artificial stone blocks. This instant building material could be cast into almost any shape and size, even to a larger scale than the stone blocks the Egyptians had used for their pyramids. Molded concrete arches were easier to build than their stone counter-

parts, which had to be put together from interlocking parts that were subject to slip out of place during construction.

Concrete had a rough, unattractive texture, however, and Roman architects were obsessed by appearance. They wanted every surface to look grand, to match their perception of their empire. So they faced concrete buildings with brick, stone, or marble veneers and inlaid walls with flashy glass-and-stone mosaics. Roman architects also disguised their buildings to imitate Greek structures. Ball comments:

[Romans] frequently annexed the structural components of Greek architecture—the column and its load—as pure surface decoration. This borrowed finery, placed judiciously on the vast Roman forms, resulted in a unique expression of magnificence wedded to power. It was so right for the circumstance of the Roman State.[14]

Thus, to make their buildings appear as splendid as they believed their empire to be, Roman architects added false Greek columns to the concrete walls of public buildings, columns strictly for looks that really did not support anything.

The Pantheon

The Pantheon, a magnificent temple dedicated to not one but seven gods, is ancient Rome's most famous architectural project. Built between A.D. 118 and 128, the Pantheon (a general term for a temple or shrine dedicated to all the gods. The word was used in Greek antiquity and carried over into the Roman era) celebrates the purest form of arch, the dome. Its format follows the typical Greek and Roman temple pattern: a porch, or portico, fronts a room enshrining statues of the gods. But

beyond the Pantheon's normal columned portico is a huge circular room over 140 feet wide, called a rotunda. The 20-foot-thick walls rise to form a cylindrical base for an enormous concrete dome. If extended to a full sphere, the dome would have touched the floor, because the rotunda's height and diameter are almost equal. The vault opened to the sky via a round window, called an oculus (eye), that let in the only light for the lavish interior. Thus, the Pantheon was transfigured daily by a shaft of sunlight circling the room with the sweeping grandeur of a celestial clock hand. The light caused the colored marble walls and floor to glow. Since the exterior was covered with bronze sheeting, the dome gleamed as well.

The spacious elegance of its interior has made the Pantheon one of the most imitated of structures. Ball describes one reason for the Pantheon's continuing impact on architecture: "Here we have one of the most restful, majestic, inwardly oriented spaces ever created by man. Only

The Pantheon is Rome's most well-known architectural contribution. A main feature is the rotunda, which has continued to be imitated by modern architects, especially when designing government structures.

The interior of the Pantheon is restful, awe-inspiring, and full of light. Its magnificent rotunda is another example of the Romans' mastery of the use of the arch.

the small oculus, or round opening 27 feet in diameter in the dome, gives any hint of the world beyond its doors."[15] The temple's shape and scale create a sanctuary for the visitor. The rotunda's entire interior is fully visible from any point in the room. While its size awes the observer, its shape inspires contemplation.

Thus, the mud-and-stone piles and bundled reeds of prehistory developed over the course of several thousand years into timeless structures like the Pantheon, which still influence architecture today. Cultures found and developed successful construction methods that provided both shelter and beauty. Architecture's challenge in the centuries to come would be to keep pace with the progress of human civilization while still expressing its unique spirit.

2 The Middle Ages

By the fourth century, the Roman Empire had begun to weaken. The empire's provinces in the Near East, such as Syria and Asia Minor, influenced the rest of the empire. Religions such as Christianity and, later, Islam soared in popularity, creating a need for a new sacred architecture. In 330, Emperor Constantine transplanted the empire's capital to Byzantium (now Istanbul), where Roman architectural styles mingled with Eastern ones. After the empire collapsed, Byzantine architecture's Eastern flavor continued to influence medieval styles to follow, such as Romanesque and Gothic.

Early Christian Architecture

The first Christian churches were converted Roman public buildings called basilicas, which featured the arched construction and vaulted ceilings common to most Roman architecture. Their layout consisted of a rectangular open space, or nave, flanked by two side aisles. An apse, or semicircular domed space, capped one or both ends. Roman judges and businessmen once gathered in basilicas. After the Roman Empire legalized Christianity in the fourth century, Christian congregations met in converted basilicas, using the nave and aisles for seating and the apse for the priest's chancel, an area containing the altar and seating for the clergy and choir. Christians chose basilicas, rather than temples, for their religious purposes because basilicas had not been tainted by use in pagan religious ceremonies.

A building originally designed for social gatherings was an appropriate choice for a Christian church. Unlike the temples of the Egyptians, Greeks, or Romans, the Christian church was not only a house of

St. Peter's Basilica is the world's largest Christian church. Originally Roman public buildings, basilicas were converted into the first Christian churches.

The interior of Old St. Peter's shows the high, open area called the transept.

God, but a home where people gathered together in communion. As Anita Abramovitz comments: "For the first time, man's path *inside* a religious building became a primary architectural consideration."[16] The basilica's design took human activity into account.

Early Christianity's foremost basilican church was St. Peter's in Rome, begun in 333. Built on Vatican Hill near the burial site of Simon Peter, one of Jesus' apostles, it served worshipers waiting to venerate the saint. It is often called Old St. Peter's to distinguish it from the grand new church of St. Peter that replaced it in the sixteenth century. Old St. Peter's unique feature was an element uncommon in its time, but typical of churches to come. Its nave did not lead directly to the domed apse. Instead, a worshiper first encountered a high, open area crossing the nave at right angles. This space, called a transept, contained small chambers at each end and was screened from the aisles by rows of columns. Beyond the transept, the apse was visible through an archway. Sixteen double windows lighted the transept, which was the focal point for religious ritual, while the rest of the church remained dim. Thus the transept had a unique, stagelike quality appropriate to the drama of early Christian ceremonies.

Byzantine Architecture

Beginning in the fourth century, Byzantine architects built upon Roman concepts. But the requirements of a Christian church were different from those of a pagan temple, as Victoria Kloss Ball explains:

> The Christian church had to accommodate laity and clergy; the pagan temple housed only the cult image. The glorification of a Greek temple was therefore on the exterior; in a

Christian sanctuary it progressed to the interior and then to a cooperative interior-exterior relationship.[17]

The Byzantines wanted to draw attention to the interior features of the church, such as the central altar, by making the surrounding structure as impressive as possible. Since they wanted to glorify God to great heights, they developed the domed church. In fact, Byzantine architects were the first to surmount the problem of placing a round dome on a square base. The Pantheon's dome rested on a cylinder, so the entire dome was in contact with its base. Putting a dome on a square base, however, would cause overhang and weaken the structure. Byzantine builders solved this problem by raising domes on pendentives, curving stone triangles that filled the space between the dome itself and the supporting masonry.

Hagia Sophia

The engineering technique incorporating pendentives was a feature of the Byzantines' greatest masterpiece, the Church of the Hagia Sophia, in Istanbul. This inspiring building, also known as the Church of Santa Sophia, was commissioned by Emperor Justinian in 532. Believing himself to be on a mission of God, he hired An-

Hagia Sophia was one of the first structures to allow a round dome to be placed on a square base with the use of pendentives, curving stone triangles that filled the space between the dome itself and the supporting masonry.

themius of Tralles, a natural scientist, and Isidore of Miletus, a physicist, to design a glittering showpiece for his architectural campaign. Marvin Trachtenberg and Isabelle Hyman explain the emperor's choice of designers:

> Justinian must have realized that only natural philosophers would be able to conceive a building of such visionary effect as he dreamed of and devise novel structural means to accomplish it. No trade-bound professional would have dared to erect such a structure, for it was not only unconventional but extremely risky.[18]

Over ten thousand workers thronged the construction site, situated where an earlier church had burned down. The emperor imported more than a hundred marble columns, plundered from old Greek and Roman temples. Thanks to Justinian's energetic backing, Hagia Sophia, a marvel of beauty and complexity, took a mere five years to complete. The result was an edifice that was overwhelming in scope. As Trachtenberg and Hyman comment: "Even the official court historian, Procopius, who watched the building go up, had trouble describing it."[19]

Hagia Sophia is nearly square, 220 feet by 250 feet. It is supported at each corner by four massive piers, or pillars, which in turn support four semicircular arches. These arches, filled in with pendentives, raise aloft a huge central dome, 107 feet in diameter, hovering 180 feet above the ground. The outside of the building is impressive in size and shape, but it is sparsely decorated. The exquisite detail was saved for the interior, the intricacy of which provides stunning contrast to the severity of the exterior.

This view of the interior of Hagia Sophia shows the small windows at the base of the dome that fill the space with light. Glittering glass mosaics and watercolor frescoes adorn the walls, inspiring awe in the worshipper.

Hagia Sophia's Interior

Ball compares Hagia Sophia's interior to the Pantheon's:

> Hagia Sophia . . . is one of the most complex and significant interior spaces in Christendom. . . . This is not the quiet space of the Pantheon, restful in its vast circular enclosure. It would almost seem that the half millennium separating the two structures had replaced too soon the quiescence of the East with the restless quality of the North and West.[20]

The cause of this restless effect was light. As Trachtenberg and Hyman explain: "The base of the dome is pierced by

The Unstable Masterpiece

In Architecture,
*Marvin Trachtenberg
and Isabelle Hyman
discuss the structural
design of the Hagia
Sophia, a brilliant
and imposing church
that is actually not as
stable as it appears to
be.*

"Brilliant in design, Hagia Sophia is not entirely secure structurally. The main piers are of exceptional solidity, built of massive . . . masonry. The rest of the building, however, was erected of brick in thick mortar beds; this technique had developed in late antiquity in Asia Minor and in its perfected form permitted firm vaulting that was wide-spanned, yet thin and light. But even if comparatively light in weight, the huge dome of Hagia Sophia generates immense thrust. Moreover, the dome is not set solidly on a massive cylindrical base, as at the Pantheon, but is perched high in the air. In the corners the thrust is absorbed by the pendentives, but what of the sides? To the east and west, the half-domes swing up to abut the dome, and the architects calculated—it now seems, correctly—that the half-domes, thin though they were, would absorb the east-west forces. The unresolved problem lay to the north and south: here the dome tottered freely in the air. Despite the massive buttressing set up at the lower levels, a great deal of 'movement' occurred above the aisles and galleries. The lateral arches, though extraordinarily deep and thick, actually were pushed outward by the immense domical pressures. The stresses set up by these distortions weakened the dome. The wonder is not that the dome, or parts of it, fell several times, but that the building still stands at all."

a ring of sizable windows so closely spaced that visually they seem to dissolve the foot of the vault into a continuous ring of light."[21] The light from these windows shimmers across the glittering glass mosaics and watercolor frescoes, or paintings in plaster, adorning the walls. The effect is one Trachtenberg terms dematerialization—the solid masses of the walls are concealed, seeming to dissolve into color,

light, and pattern. Ball believes this lighting effect heralds contemporary architecture: "This great building with its myriad candles of light flickering through its many small windows and its reflections from glass mosaics and resplendent metals anticipated designing through light."[22]

The special ornamental carving on the marble walls, called incrustation, is another detail that emphasizes Hagia

Sophia's dramatic lighting. In this technique, which originated in ancient Syria, the artist uses a primitive drill on the soft marble, rather than a chisel, to make deep grooves called undercuts. The resulting ornamental carving has sharp edges that cast bold shadows. Incrustation gave the walls a delicate, lacy texture, and the interplay of light and dark made the walls appear to sparkle.

Thus, the massive exterior of Hagia Sophia seems to dissolve, ghostlike, before the eyes of awestruck visitors. The structural necessity of hoisting the heavy dome above its rectangular base resulted in the church's mysterious beauty. Trachtenberg and Hyman explain the effect on the observer:

> In Hagia Sophia, the observer's position and perceptions are never clear. . . . The great vault does not reach down to enfold one at the center, but floats impossibly high, a distant, symbolic vision of a perfection unattainable in this life—truly, as Procopius wrote, "A golden dome suspended from Heaven."[23]

Romanesque Architecture

After the fall of the Roman Empire around the end of the fifth century, European civilization plunged downhill, losing its wealth and influence. Art and culture were forgotten: Few monuments were built between 500 and 700. Many of the engineering feats developed by the Romans—such as large-scale vaulting, concrete construction, and decorative arts such as mosaic and carving—disappeared in the course of a few generations.

After Charlemagne was crowned emperor of the Holy Roman Empire in 800, architecture in Europe experienced a brief upswing. A few imposing buildings, such as France's Palatine Chapel (796–805), went up in a campaign to renew European civilization's glory. The revitalization did not last long, however. After Charlemagne's death in 814, a backlash of violence and terror descended on Europe, which was invaded and plundered by Slavs, Magyars, Arabs, and Vikings. Neither people nor buildings

The Palatine Chapel of Charlemagne was one of the few monumental structures built from 500 to 800.

Living Architecture

In Architecture and Interior Design, *art historian Victoria Kloss Ball describes the organic quality of Romanesque architecture, explaining that its similarity to a living organism makes it a forerunner of both Gothic and modern architecture.*

"Following Charlemagne's reign [800–814], the widespread destruction of buildings at the hands of the Norse and Slavic firebrands posed the problem of restoration in a more durable manner. Masonry and vaulted roofs were thus the first characteristics of important Romanesque church architecture. . . .

The everyday skill in vault construction possessed by the Romans was relearned so that it was again possible to roof wide church naves with groin vaults. A further development was the rib vault in which the framework of diagonally arched ribs is independently constructed. This has the advantage of economy of centering during construction, of light cell structure, hence greater space potential, and of the possibility of opening a window area because the rib skeleton is largely load bearing and the walls as supporting members can be partially eliminated. . . .

Anyone who thoughtfully considers these innovations which were the work of eleventh century engineer-masons appreciates that here a structural principle was evolving to a degree that could merit a new name. If the lines of stress, carried along the groins, or later along the ribs, are countered by buttressing at strategic points, then the system becomes like a living organism, whose forces oppose one another, and the connecting membrane decreases in importance in its effect on stability. The term organic, with its suggested analogy to living organisms, is appropriate because in an organic body the thrusts and counterthrusts with their accompanying tensions operate quite independently of the inert flesh that covers the skeleton. In respect to its structure this normative Romanesque architecture is a direct antecedent of the Gothic and both are heralds of much that is built today."

were safe. Churches were favorite targets for looters, since treasures were often stored within, and many were destroyed.

Amazingly, Europe survived. By the tenth century, the invading cultures had either integrated with the European or moved on. Political upheaval gave way to economic growth. Business prospered, and with it came a cultural revival and a new hope and spirituality. The surge of religious enthusiasm inspired a new interest in church building. In this climate, in the eleventh century, the Romanesque style of architecture was born.

Western Europe of 150 to 1200 was a feudalistic society; that is, there were few cities, and most people lived under the protection of the lords and abbots of scattered castles and monasteries. These buildings were designed in the Romanesque style. Because they were fortresses, Romanesque structures were heavy. The earlier Romanesque buildings were also somewhat crudely constructed, because the workers were unskilled. By the 1100s, however, Romanesque architects had achieved mastery. The most beautiful and technically innovative Romanesque structures were churches.

A Romanesque church was built in the shape of a Latin cross, which has one short arm and one long arm. The curved stone roofs, or vaults, were supported by heavy columns and thick walls. The round arches were decorated with carved figures and frescoes, or paintings in plaster, of religious scenes. These decorations, a characteristic feature of Romanesque churches, served to brighten them somewhat. Because of the heavy roof load they carried, most Romanesque churches were dark, low buildings, their walls relieved with only the narrowest of windows. Later Romanesque architects attempted to adjust for this design problem by using new building methods.

Romanesque architecture featured the round arches and barrel vaults used by the Romans. Architects focused on transform-

The Romanesque style Basilica de la Madalaine Vezelay is a good example of the use of barrel vaults.

ing the early Christian basilicas, with their long side aisles and high naves (main passages) into bigger, taller, more complex structures, fit to express religious fervor. And, naturally, after seeing countless wooden-roofed churches burned by invaders, they wanted a structure that would last. Romanesque architects had ambition, but they also needed to develop technical skills to solve the structural riddles they had posed for themselves.

The architects of the Romanesque period developed techniques that helped them achieve bigger buildings that still had grace and delicacy. First, they countered the crushing weight of stone roofs with clustered piers, or columns, instead of single supporting columns. The

The Basilica de la Madalaine Vezelay features clustered arches, which were needed to hold the weight of the newly invented stone roof.

tendency for a building to give in to sideways pressure from the heavy roof was counteracted by buttresses, extra supports that reinforced the walls from the outside. Rib vaults, which were skeletal arches that followed the shape of the roof vaulting, provided additional support while managing to give a lightweight appearance.

The Pisa Cathedral

As it developed, the Romanesque style broke up into various regional styles, all equally adventurous. A church well known today for its famous leaning tower, the cathedral of Pisa, represents an Italian regional Romanesque style called Tuscan Romanesque. In Pisa, Tuscan Romanesque is characterized by extensive use of arcades, or rows of arches supported on columns.

The cathedral of Pisa and its surrounding buildings were built in the eleventh century, when the city-state of Pisa was a great sea power. In celebration of a victory against the Saracens, the Pisans began construction of the cathedral in 1063. It was not completed until the thirteenth century. In keeping with Romanesque tradition, its form was that of an early Christian basilica, but on a far grander scale. The nave contains five aisles, the transept three aisles. An oval dome rises over the intersection of the cross-shaped building.

The Pisa cathedral, an example of Tuscan Romanesque architecture, makes extensive use of arcades—rows of arches supported on columns.

The cathedral's interior is complex and spacious, and the walls are striped with bands of colored marble. These patterns are partly screened by blind arcading (false arcades applied to walls as decoration). The layering gives the walls a multicolored, textured effect similar to richly patterned fabric. On the outside, the cathedral repeats the pattern of arcading. On the west facade, or front wall, rows of stacked arcades stretch upward, veiling the supporting wall with an airy web of slender columns.

The freestanding bell tower at Pisa is a monument that generates great local pride. Like the other buildings surrounding the cathedral of Pisa, its design picks up elements from the building itself. Its tiers of delicate arcading resemble the rows of arcades on the cathedral facade. Trachtenberg and Hyman explain the tower's appeal:

Although famed as the Leaning Tower, the structure's principal virtue is not its perilous inclination (due to faulty subsoil). Even if perfectly in plumb, the graceful and harmonious Campanile would be the world's most beautiful bell tower (although it would lose its telling pathos). Structurally, it is no more than a transformation of the flat cathedral facade into cylindrical form, but the ingenious operation was accomplished with great aesthetic skill. The solid base supports six tiers of open arcading, poised lacelike around the shadowed, cylindrical supporting wall.[24]

Romanesque architecture, then, progressed from low, dark, nearly windowless buildings to the rich, delicate, lacelike

The leaning tower of Pisa repeats the pattern of stacked arcades found inside. The tower leans not by design, but because of the faulty soil upon which it rests.

quality of the cathedral of Pisa and other late Romanesque structures. However, the accomplishments of Romanesque architects would be surpassed by those of the architects of the Gothic style to come.

This movement, which began in the 1200s, resulted in a higher, brighter church. Gothic cathedrals could not have evolved without the experimentation with rib vaulting and other methods contributed by Romanesque architects. But the beauty and technical innovation the Gothic period achieved was truly miraculous. Meanwhile, over the course of centuries, the medieval followers of another religion, Islam, were achieving architectural miracles of their own.

3 Islam's Influence and Gothic Architecture

After the death of the prophet Mohammed in 632, the new religion of Islam swept across Arabia to reach India, China, North Africa, and Spain. Building in conquered cities, Moslems began to create an architectural tradition of their own that parallels that of Western civilization, with which it shares many features: large interior spaces, domed ceilings, columns, and arches. But drawing from these same forms, Islam created a unique style during the thousand years its architecture flowered.

Islamic Architecture

The Blue Mosque in Istanbul sports a typical sixteenth-century feature—a main dome surrounded by smaller domes.

The Mosque

The temple and the cathedral find their Islamic counterpart in the mosque. The typical eighth-century mosque was laid out for the same purpose as the Roman basilica, as a place of assembly. The building was used for prayer and religious instruction, and it was always oriented toward the city of Mecca, Mohammed's birthplace. Mosques were rectangular and included an open inner courtyard surrounded by arcaded galleries, or upper-story corridors. Many mosques were constructed on the sites of ruined Roman temples and incorporated parts of the original marble foundations.

As centuries of development unfolded, the mosque changed appearance. A typical sixteenth-century mosque was domi-

The courtyard of the Alhambra, an Islamic palace in Granada, Spain, imitates the homes of wealthy Greeks and Romans.

nated by a unifying central dome, surrounded by a cluster of smaller domes. The structure's most characteristic features were its tall tapering minarets, one at each corner. A minaret is a balconied tower from which Moslems are called to prayer. One of Islamic architecture's few vertical forms, the minaret is a recognizable symbol to Moslems of their faith, functioning in the way the cross typically does for Christians.

On the inside, Moslem buildings were richly ornamented. According to Trachtenberg and Hyman, their architectural decoration was meant to inspire viewers to forget they were inside a mere building:

> [O]ne of the functions of pervasive ornamental decoration in Muslim buildings was to obscure intentionally [the] clarity of form and . . . organization, and to achieve through the repetition of interlocking shapes—all-enclosing and without rhythmic interruption or a definition of parts—a hypnotic trancelike mood or spiritual transport

conducive to prayer and to communal meditation of the . . . nature of Islam.[25]

Thus, an Islamic structure served as a religious symbol, reminding its occupant that there was a divine world beyond its mesmerizing material walls.

The Alhambra

Two great Islamic architectural projects, the Alhambra palace in Granada, Spain, and the Taj Mahal mausoleum in Agra, India, are separated by several centuries. The Alhambra, begun in the thirteenth century, took about one hundred years to complete. This magnificent palace is actually a sprawling city containing a palace, a mosque, and baths. Its Lion Court, a courtyard of reflecting ponds and fountains fronted by heavy arcades on exceptionally thin columns, is patterned after descriptions of paradise in Islamic poetry. The courtyard also harks back to the columned courtyards in the wealthy Greek and Roman homes of antiquity.

The Alhambra: Paradise on Earth

In The Ascent of Man, *scholar Jacob Bronowski describes the Alhambra as the last and most exquisite Arab monument.*

"Seen from the outside, the Alhambra is a square, brutal fortress that does not hint at Arab forms. Inside, it is not a fortress but a palace, and a palace designed deliberately to prefigure on earth the bliss of heaven. The Alhambra is a late construction. It has the lassitude [listnessnesss] of an empire past its peak, unadventurous and, it thought, safe. The religion of meditation has become sensuous and self-satisfied. It sounds with the music of water, whose sinuous line runs through all Arab melodies. . . . Each court in turn is the echo and the memory of a dream, through which the Sultan floated (for he did not walk, he was carried). The Alhambra is most nearly the description of Paradise from the Koran [Islamic sacred writings]. . . .

The Alhambra is the last and most exquisite monument of Arab civilisation in Europe. The last Moorish king reigned here until 1492, when Queen Isabella of Spain was already backing the adventure of Columbus. It is a honeycomb of courts and chambers, and the Sala de las Camas is the most secret place in the palace. Here the girls from the harem came after the bath and reclined, naked. Blind musicians played in the gallery, the eunuchs padded about. And the Sultan watched from above, and sent an apple down to signal to the girl of his choice that she would spend the night with him.

In a western civilisation, this room would be filled with marvellous drawings of the female form, erotic pictures. Not so here. The representation of the human body was forbidden to Mohammedans. Indeed, even the study of anatomy at all was forbidden, and that was a major handicap to Moslem science. So here we find coloured but extraordinarily simple geometric designs. The artist and the mathematician in Arab civilisation have become one."

A stunning and significant feature of the Alhambra is a unique type of decoration called *muqarnas* work. According to Trachtenberg and Hyman, *muqarnas* originated in North Africa and is one of Moslem architecture's great contributions:

A type of three-dimensional architectural decoration formed by stucco, or sometimes wood, into a multiple network of open cells, *muqarnas* resembles the cross-section of a honeycomb. . . . It covers entirely the structural organization beneath the surface of a wall or vault, which appears to have been "scooped out" in the process of forming this uniquely rich cellular overlay.[26]

The Taj Mahal

Islamic architecture achieved a high point of harmony and nobility in the world-famous Taj Mahal ("Crown of the Palace") (1631-1648), a white marble monument built by Shah Jehan as a tomb for himself and his wife. The majestic structure features the domes and minarets that had become Islamic architecture's trademarks. Like the Alhambra, the Taj Mahal's ornamental pools and gardens echo literary descriptions of paradise. The Taj Mahal's dome swells from a cube base inlaid with decorative stonework. Needle-sharp minarets stand apart from the structure, each separately silhouetted against the sky.

Perhaps the most well-known example of Islamic architecture is the Taj Mahal. The building is a study in symmetry, with identical minarets rising along the sides of the main structure.

In the Taj Mahal, empty space and solid mass are in perfect balance, the outcome of ten centuries of Moslem architectural achievement. Its design combines the opulence and dreamlike nature of the Islamic tradition with the classic poise and symmetry of the West.

Gothic Architecture

In the eleventh, twelfth, and thirteenth centuries, architects of the Romanesque style had begun to grapple with the technical challenges of building a tall, graceful, yet indestructible stone church. The architectural period later known as

In this view of Rheims cathedral in France, the classic rib vaults found in Gothic style architecture are clearly seen.

Gothic, dating from about 1150 and continuing through about 1550, succeeded in meeting these challenges with unforgettable flair and drama.

The Gothic style originated in twelfth-century France, which is why it was originally known as *opus francigenum,* or "French work." It copied much from styles that came before, reorganizing the borrowed details into a unique, exciting form, the Gothic cathedral. The Gothic style is characterized by rib vaults, pointed arches, and flying buttresses. These techniques created a thrusting, soaring effect, almost as if the cathedral were in midflight.

The Pointed Arch

Pointed arches had been used in Syria and Mesopotamia, and later in some Romanesque architecture. But they were not fully taken advantage of until the beginning of the Gothic movement. The pointed arch solved the problem of covering large churches with strong stone roofs by improving on the earlier rounded arch. Rounded arches were limited to forming barrel-vaulted roofs. Their height was dictated by the distance to be covered: a large distance meant an excessively high vault. Writer George Sullivan explains the advantages of the pointed arch over the rounded arch as a roof covering:

> The problem had a simple solution: point the arch. The pointed arch could be adjusted to any height the architect wished, so the distance being spanned was of no great significance. And since its sides approached the vertical, it exerted much less outward thrust than a rounded arch of equal span. The pointed arch thus gave architects a

A New Faith

In People and Spaces, *writer Anita Abramovitz discusses the social climate of the Middle Ages, which gave birth to the Gothic style.*

"When Gothic was born about the middle of the twelfth century, it came into a world still controlled by feudal power, a world of princely lands and scattered duchies that had not yet coalesced into the nations of Europe. Just as the rounded arch forms were beginning to give way to pointed arches and ever-heightening vaulted spaces, so was a more modern world beginning to flower and expand. From our point of view, the Middle Ages may not seem so free and and modern, but, compared with monastic Dark Ages, a whole new spirit was abroad. A middle class was emerging, caught up in trade and commerce. All was movement and diversification, but also belief in permanence and unity, wisdom and authority apart form everyday existence, which was limited and beset by all kinds of immediate problems. There must have been a yearning to believe in unlimited possibilities; it was a time of growth for a new faith (Christianity), a new system, a new spirit and function, and the cathedral can be seen as a synthesis of these new attitudes. There was a rhythm of movement, of searching, of reaching out in the world, a dramatic conflict of thrust and counteraction that one likes to think is reflected in the rhythm of the cathedrals with their changeable sequences of complex spaces, differing heights, and soaring verticals."

flexibility and freedom in design that they had never before enjoyed.[27]

The pointed arch was not only sturdy and versatile, it was exciting and dynamic, giving to a structure a lively energy that could not be achieved by the restful, static rounded arch. This dramatic quality appealed to Gothic architects, who wanted their churches to reflect the joy they derived from their Christian faith.

The Flying Buttress

Flying buttresses are another one of the unusual features that give Gothic architecture an almost living quality of motion and rhythm. According to Anita Abramovitz, "Buttresses can be understood this way: imagine propping up a row of books at either end. Ideal bookends would be long-based, heavy, right-angled

Notre-Dame Cathedral is an excellent example of both the use of flying buttresses and tracery, which strengthens the glass windows.

triangles, the right-angled side holding back the thrust of the books."[28] A flying buttress is so called because of the way its arc leaps over space, seeming to fly up to the building it presses against. Since flying buttresses took on much of the weight of Gothic cathedrals, walls could become lightweight networks of translucent windows, allowing architects freedom to paint with light and color. Thanks to thinner walls supported by buttresses, cathedrals glowed from the filtered light of stained glass windows. The windows were strengthened by tracery, or branching, openwork dividers of thin stone that formed petal-like patterns against the glass.

Flying buttresses act as a kind of skeletal framework. They form an extension of the building's internal support network of vault and column, and reveal the inner structure of the cathedral to the observer outside the building. Ball compares the structure of a Gothic cathedral to the flesh and bone of a living creature: "[R]ib vaults, pointed arches, flying buttresses, all [were] used to attain such a carefully planned system of counterthrusts that equipoise [a state of balance] seemed the function of the linear skeleton, to which a membrane was affixed."[29] Like the human body, the Gothic church's skeleton of arch and buttress gives strength and balance to the building's thin, skinlike walls. The Gothic style's skeletal framework was a forerunner of the steel skeleton of the modern skyscraper.

Because of the balancing of tensions made possible by the pointed arch and the flying buttress, Gothic cathedrals seemed to soar heavenward. Architects emphasized the vertical thrust by topping the buttresses with pinnacles, small towers with pointed roofs. Although decorative, the pinnacles also served the practical

The stained glass windows at Chartres were made entirely by hand. Although glass was stained before the Gothic period, stained glass windows could not be used until advances in architectural design allowed for them.

purpose of adding weight to make the buttresses stronger. Spires, or pointed tops on roofs or towers, also reached skyward.

Stained Glass Windows

Another structural innovation that contributed to the magical lighting effects of Gothic cathedrals was not totally new. The craft of staining glass with color is an ancient one. However, churches of the Romanesque period found little chance to use it, since to keep the walls strong enough to support heavy roofs, only small, narrow windows could be used. The complex structural support system of the Gothic style, with its balances and counterbalances, made the liberal use of windows a possibility for the first time. With the windows came light, flooding into the houses of worship like a blessing.

Glass in medieval times was tinted, baked, and smoothed by hand. As a result, it contained imperfections such as bubbles and ripples that enhanced its beauty: The flaws in the stained glass, as well as the lovely tints of the glass itself, caught the shafts of sun penetrating the cathedral in patterns that changed with the changing light outside. Thus the handcrafted windows gave each cathedral a unique beauty.

Stained glass windows were expensive to make, so it was traditional for noblemen to donate windows to churches. It became customary, as well, for wealthy donors to request that their own images be represented in smaller stained glass panels beneath the main windows. Guilds of workers also pitched in funds for the building of their towns' cathedrals, and stained glass panels illustrating various crafts (blacksmith, carpenter, etc.) similarly were incorporated into a larger window design. Such personal touches give Gothic cathedrals part of their individuality and show the spirit of cooperation in which they were built.

The rose window was the most elaborate stained glass design, and the most difficult one to make. Rose windows are huge, circular windows designed to suggest the petals of a full-blown rose. The effect is a design of great delicacy worked in the heavy medium of stone.

Tracery

Rose windows as well as other stained glass designs were held together by tracery, a framework of thin stone bars dividing large stained glass panels into smaller units. This web of supporting stonework was necessary to allow the craftsman to set the sections of the windows in place easily and to keep them from sagging. Tracery typically formed narrow, arching shapes at the bottom portions of large windows. The top portions were ornamented with tracery in the forms of circles and crescents. Tracery contributed to the delicacy of the windows and greatly added to a cathedral's majesty. In its later stages, tracery lost its geometric look and took on a flowing appearance. This style was called flamboyant (from "flame") because the outlines it traced on the window resembled flames.

Rheims Cathedral

Famous French cathedrals that embody the tension between opposing forces and the rhythmic upward movement of the Gothic style include Chartres (1194–1260), Rheims (1211–mid-1400s), Notre-Dame (about 1000–1250), and Amiens (about 1220–1269). Sullivan describes Rheims:

> The interior is breathtaking, with vertical lines dominating throughout. The array of pointed arches high above the nave arcades, the upward thrust of the evenly spaced supporting shafts, and the slender ribs of stone which transmit the vault weights to thin columns—all of these lead the eye upward. Toward the end of the fifteenth

century, Charles VIII called Rheims "the noblest of all churches in the Kingdom of France."[30]

Chartres Cathedral

Throughout its history, the cathedral of Chartres has been linked with the Virgin Mary, who is considered its patron saint. In 876, before it was rebuilt in the Gothic style, Chartres received the gift of a holy relic from Charles the Bald, Charlemagne's grandson. This relic was a red tunic said to have been worn by the Virgin Mary at the time of her death. The relic was cherished by the people of Chartres, but it was stolen by invading Normans a generation later. Furious, the French recaptured the treasure and made a gold and cedar box for it. The box was hidden inside the church, and the church became known as "Our Lady of Chartres."

Thus the Chartres cathedral was already rich in history when a fire in 1134 destroyed its western facade. This was rebuilt in the 1140s. However, another fire, in 1194, burned the entire church to its foundations. (The relic of the Virgin Mary was safely buried in the foundations and escaped damage.) The second fire created the opportunity for the townspeople to rebuild their beloved cathedral in the grand new architectural mode. The Gothic Chartres cathedral was completed in 1260.

The Chartres cathedral was rebuilt when the Gothic style was in full bloom, and the townspeople were eager to see fashionable structural elements, such as flying buttresses, adorn their church. The west facade of Chartres reflects the development of the Gothic architectural style. Its three arched doorways crowned by

The cathedral of Chartres was destroyed by a fire in 1194. It was rebuilt in Gothic style.

cade. This spire, designed in the fancy, late Gothic style, does not match the plainer south spire, but it does not look out of place.

The soaring spires of the Chartres cathedral are visible from miles away, dwarfing the crowded buildings of the town clustered in the church's shadow. The entire structure presents an elegant blend of centuries of effort and creativity, a triumphant example of Gothic cathedral architecture.

The rise of the Gothic cathedral during the twelfth and thirteenth centuries was a source of pride to Europeans. The number of cathedrals built was remarkable. Even smaller cities competed to erect large churches, which were paid for by the bishops. At Chartres, although the actual construction was done by skilled masons, the townspeople helped haul stones to the building site.

The people for whom the cathedrals were built no doubt recognized the technical skill as well as the religious feeling that went into their conception and execution. It is ironic that the Renaissance Italians considered the Middle Ages barbaric, terming the style of the pointed arch "Gothic," or savage. In fact, the Middle Ages were not a thousand years of darkness following the fall of Rome, but a millennium of imagination and exploration that paved the way for the more sophisticated and scientific Renaissance civilization to follow.

arched windows date from the twelfth century, as does the south spire, or tower. But the builders did not stop with these adornments. In the thirteenth century, a magnificent rose window was added to the facade. Then, in the 1500s, a second spire was built at the north corner of the fa-

4 Renaissance and Baroque Architecture

The period known as the Renaissance, which means "rebirth," was a time of radical change in art, religion, and humanity. The Renaissance began in the fourteenth century and continued through the fifteenth and sixteenth centuries. Society today is still under the influence of the changes wrought by the Renaissance.

Renaissance Architecture

The Renaissance style of architecture began in Italy. Architects began to imitate the classical building styles of the ancient Greeks and Romans. Architects of the period were often sculptors, painters, clocksmiths, engineers, scientists, and mathematicians as well as building designers. Italian Renaissance architects often counseled architects in the royal courts of other European countries, and the Renaissance style soon spread throughout the Continent.

Architects of the Renaissance did not merely copy earlier classical forms. They created new forms of their own, using classical styles as inspiration. Versatility and boldness characterized their churches, palaces, and other public buildings. Their efforts were backed by wealthy royal courts and popes.

According to Ball, Renaissance architects thought that the way a building looked was more important artistically than its actual structure:

> The Renaissance architect did not hesitate to cover joints with stucco or indeed to create false ones . . . and he shamelessly and without disguise used tie rods and chains to strengthen arches, vaults, and domes. He painted an architectural grid of classical orders on facades when it suited his purpose. This "outrageous" behavior was not the result of ignorance on his part; it was in deference to a principle that seemed more important in his eyes—the visual formalizing principle. How a thing looked was of more consequence than any disclosure of the logic of its construction.[31]

Renaissance architecture, then, did not object to presenting a false front. Architects added fake columns and other historically inspired decoration to their own more technically advanced buildings. They honored Greek and Roman architecture by imitating its appearance without resurrecting its unsophisticated structure.

The Cathedral of Santa Maria del Fiore

The great dome of the cathedral of Santa Maria del Fiore represents the concealment of inner workings for the sake of outer appearance. It also is an impressive example of Renaissance architecture's early technical contribution, called "the dome on a drum."

Santa Maria del Fiore, the cathedral of Florence, was begun during the Middle Ages, but construction halted before completion. An eight-sided drum surrounded its large central crossing. This drum was meant to have been crowned by a dome. Filippo Brunelleschi, a sculptor and goldsmith who was also versed in mechanical engineering and mathematics, was given the important assignment of completing the cathedral in 1418.

Brunelleschi had studied Roman architecture, especially the Pantheon and its great dome. However, while he made use of the classic Roman arch and vault, he did so in a unique and original manner. The Romans had never domed an octagonal drum. Brunelleschi met this challenge with a combination of techniques, including the Gothic method of stone ribbing. Structural ribs were concealed inside and outside the dome for added strength.

Brunelleschi's innovative dome had several parts. Its lower portion was octagonal to fit its base, but the top part of the dome was circular, capping the eight-sided bottom portion. Brunelleshi accomplished his feat of placing a circle on an octagon through complicated geometry and mechanics that are still being investigated. Additionally, his entire ribbed dome had a double shell of stone and brick. Narrow stairs, concealed within the

The great Italian architect Brunelleschi propelled architecture forward when he designed the dome of the cathedral of Santa Maria del Fiore to rest on an octagonal base.

dome's sandwiched layers, allowed workers to enter the space between the shells to perform safety checks and repairs.

According to Trachtenberg and Hyman, Brunelleschi's dome was an exciting breakthrough. The architect's contemporaries in Florence recognized it and took pride in it: "Brunelleschi had invented a new technological system for the construction of the prescribed Gothic design of the dome, and by so doing had left behind the medieval world to which that design belonged."[32] Brunelleschi's famous "Duomo," as it is nicknamed, propelled Renaissance architecture toward the future.

The Tempietto

In the early sixteenth century, Rome replaced Florence as Italy's architectural center. One of Rome's great Renaissance architects was Donato Bramante, who in 1502 was assigned to design a memorial to Saint Peter in the cloistered courtyard of Rome's church of San Pietro. According to Ball, the small-scale memorial was both classically balanced and emotionally moving, a perfect model for the High Renaissance style: "The Tempietto, or little temple, is undoubtedly the gem of High Italian Renaissance architecture. . . . At this point the High Renaissance had arrived."[33]

The Tempietto is round, similar to a Roman temple. A columned porch encircles the thick-walled cella, or inner room. Bramante designed it to be visible from all sides. In fact, his original plan called for

Bramante's Tempietto is too small to hold a congregation. The little building is more like a piece of art in Renaissance style than a functional temple.

Architect Donato Bramante worked during the Renaissance. His buildings are still admired for their beauty and innovation.

the monument to be surrounded by a ring of columns. Instead, however, the Tempietto had to be located in an enclosed courtyard. Bramante thought of the little building as a piece of artwork to be admired rather than a place to be entered, as Trachtenberg and Hyman point out: "The building, too small on the inside to accommodate a congregation (only 15 feet in diameter), was conceived as a 'picture' to be looked at from outside, a 'marker,' a symbol of Saint Peter's martyrdom."[34]

The charming, beautifully proportioned building is not an exact copy of a Roman temple. For one thing, its height is twice its width, which was unheard-of in Roman temple design. In addition, its dome is elevated on a tall drum. This, too, was Bramante's own idea. Bramante also experimented with light and shade in a way that was unique to the Renaissance. Following Leonardo da Vinci's ideas about the role of light in sculpture, the architect harnessed the play of sunlight, "painting" with light to show the temple walls' thick contours.

St. Peter's Basilica

Bramante's Tempietto previewed his greatest, final project, the rebuilding of St. Peter's Basilica. The original church of St. Peter's in Rome was an early Christian conversion of an ancient Roman basilica, or public meeting hall. In the early sixteenth century, an ambitious pope, Julius II, decided to tear down the old basilica and replace it with a grand new church. His decision resulted in what is now the largest Christian church in the world.

Bramante was given the honor of taking charge of the important project in 1506, and he drew the initial plans, but he died only a few years later. Other giants of the Renaissance, including the famous sculptor Michelangelo, continued the work until the church was finally completed 150 years later.

Even though he was only briefly involved with the project, Bramante's daring design for St. Peter's Basilica influenced church architecture throughout Europe for the rest of the century. The classically inspired size and shape became the hallmark for nearly every sixteenth-century church to follow, according to Trachtenberg and Hyman:

> Few sixteenth-century churches failed to include at least some of the salient features of Bramante's building: the Greek cross; the gigantic canted piers with their paired pilaster order and deep niches; the wells of space united through arched openings; the barrel vaults; and the fluid shapes of the

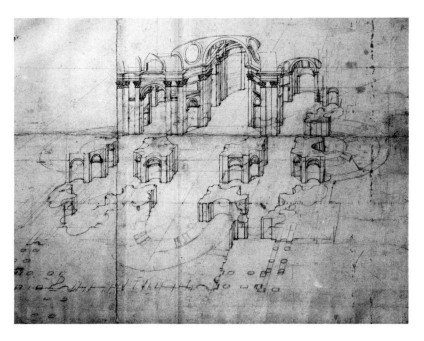

Bramante died before he could complete his plan to rebuild St. Peter's Basilica. Michelangelo would later return to Bramante's plans when he took over the job 150 years later.

heavy masonry. Equally effective was the restitution of the heroic scale of the ancient buildings from which Bramante learned so much about the Empire that was lost but could be regained.[35]

Bramante had planned a low dome for St. Peter's, similar to the Pantheon's semicircular dome. When Michelangelo took over, however, he called for a towering, steeply sloped dome that would dominate the skyline and signal to the world the authority of the church, which was being challenged by Protestantism. Michelangelo himself did not live to see the finished dome, but he left a model to guide architects who followed. Sullivan describes Michelangelo's dome:

The dome of St. Peter's, designed by Michelangelo, is one of the most imitated structures in the world.

The supporting masonry had been completed in the form of a square. Michelangelo reinforced the main piers around the square. Then, using pendentives, [he] set a high drum atop the square. The dome itself, springing from the drum, was built in the form of two shells, the interior one an almost perfect hemisphere, and the exterior one raised to a pointed oval and crowned (like Brunelleschi's Santa Maria del Fiore at Florence) with a great stone lantern, a tall windowed turret.[36]

Baroque Architecture

St. Peter's Basilica expresses the noble spirit of Renaissance architecture. However, the pomp and splendor of the Renaissance was soon challenged by a more eccentric, less dignified, but still luxurious style called baroque. The baroque style rebelled against the cool reasonableness of Renaissance classicism. Its architects reveled in creating emotional, dramatic effects that startled the viewer, as Anita Abramovitz comments:

The absolute devotion to classic disciplines—scale, proportion, and rules—which had been an essential part of early Renaissance design gradually gave way to the urgencies of imagination and self-expression and to the desire to evoke an emotional response in the viewer. . . . [A]rchitects became more and more fascinated with the illusionary possibilities of perspective and the drama of the unexpected, as against the rational and disciplined.[37]

Baroque Breaks the Rules

Anita Abramovitz explains in People and Spaces *how the volatile political climate of the seventeenth century provoked an extreme reaction in the birth of baroque architecture.*

"Just as the Renaissance was a time of competition and conflicts between artists and patrons, it was also a time for conflicts among nations, and these often led, in the later part of the Renaissance, to wars. During the seventeenth century there was the Thirty Years' War (1618–1648); the Puritan Revolution of 1642 in England, and constant religious conflict which came to a head in the Reformation and the Counter-Reformation. It was a century of discovery, geographical and scientific. The world continued to widen fast. It was both rich, restless, and excessive; poor, wretched, and fanatical. It is not surprising that architecture, too, eventually began to break with the past—distort, alter, and remodel old forms. The bonds of classic discipline broke completely when most Renaissance architecture after Michelangelo exploded into the Baroque. The Baroque architect threw away the rule book, the classic measurements, restraints, and all the precepts. . . .

Baroque at its height represented self-expression gone wild: *pediments* (the triangular form used over windows and doors in classic design), cornices, *entablatures* (beams), moldings, and columns were twisted, broken, reformed, duplicated, and decorated in later Baroque (called *Rococo*) with carved statues of saints, angels, and especially cherubs. These prolific denizens of Rococo-Baroque are poised on every pedestal, peer from every cornice, and hover like birds from heaven on swooping, curving moldings, a world removed from the pure, straight lines of the classic forms. . . . It is obvious that these buildings were not designed to be comprehended intellectually. All interior space, in scale, which was grandiose, in dramatic effects of light and shadow, and in unexpected and often overwhelming decoration, was concentrated on producing a sensational emotional effect."

The term *baroque* comes from "barroco," a Portuguese word for an irregularly shaped pearl. It is the architecture of the curved line, not the straight one. Columns and other architectural elements that in the Renaissance style marched regularly across building facades were broken, twisted, or garishly decorated with scrolls, cherubs, shells, and foliage in the baroque style. Its many critics used "baroque" as an insult, charging that its explosive ornamentation made the style ridiculous. But baroque architects wanted to pique the interest of their viewers. Surprising and often overwhelming, baroque buildings provoked strong emotional reactions.

The church of Sant'Andrea al Quirinale is entirely oval, typifying the use of the curved line popularized during the baroque period.

The intensity of baroque architecture, its flagrant demand for attention, resulted from the sixteenth-century political climate. George Sullivan supplies the historical context:

Socially and politically, the sixteenth century was a time of conflict and contrast. Europe's tranquillity was shattered by the Protestant Reformation. The Counter Reformation, the reactive movement of the Roman Catholic Church, was accompanied by an upsurge in church-building. In Spain and France, temporal rule become concentrated in the hands of the kings, and every branch of art was called upon to glorify and give testimony to regal power and eminence.[38]

Baroque buildings, then, shouted out in loud and gaudy style the supremacy of the ruling class. But more than just symbols of royal or ecclesiastical power, they were masterpieces of showmanship.

Church of Sant'Andrea al Quirinale

The oval has been called the plaything of the baroque architect. One famous church, Sant'Andrea al Quirinale in Rome, is entirely oval. Begun in 1658 and completed in 1670, it was designed by Gianlorenzo Bernini, a brilliant sculptor, architect, playwright, and stage designer. His talent for theater was apparent in the drama of his famous architectural works.

His oval church features a dramatic facade placed on one of the short ends of the oval. Above the entrance, a marble figure of Saint Andrew, winging toward heaven and trailing clouds, thrusts toward the viewer. The sculpture of Saint Andrew is surrounded by colored marbles and gilding. This dramatic facade has the quality of a religious vision brought to life for the visitor.

The Cornaro Chapel

Bernini's Cornaro Chapel is even more theatrical, almost like a play carved in stone. The chapel was designed as part of the church of Santa Maria della Vittoria (1645–1652) for the Cornaro family of Rome. It is Bernini's reenactment of a mystical vision experienced by Saint Theresa of Avila. According to Trachtenberg and Hyman: "The Cornaro Chapel is one of the most dynamic multimedia complexes in Roman Baroque art, and represents a powerful fusion of sculpture, architecture, painting, and stagecraft."[39]

Inside the Cornaro Chapel, a projecting oval niche serves as a stage for the sculpture. On it, Bernini uses the figures of a saint and an angel carved in marble to recreate the moment when Saint Theresa's heart was pierced by the arrow of divine love. On the chapel walls surrounding the scene, marble figures representing the Cornaro family watch and discuss the miracle as if they were an audience in a celestial theater. The upper walls and ceiling are painted to look like a heavenly sky of billowing clouds. A strategically placed window floods the illusion in light.

Thus the chapel becomes a backdrop for the drama of religious fervor that Bernini staged for his audience of worshipers.

The Fountain of Trevi

The drama of the baroque style continued to influence architecture of the eigh-

The statue of Saint Theresa at the Cornaro Chapel is placed on a stagelike platform. A viewer of the statue is given the impression that a story is unfolding, just as in a theater performance.

teenth century. One of Rome's most appealing tourist attractions today is a charming example of the baroque style's theatricality. The Fountain of Trevi (1732–1762) was designed by Nicola Salvi as a city planning project. The monument resembles a palace facade, almost like an elaborate stage set. The fake facade is adorned with a classical-style triumphal archway and a row of pillars. Piled in front, stones cut to look like natural rock carry on the baroque illusion. The fountain itself is a technical as well as an

The Fountain of Trevi typifies the ornate style of the baroque. Designed by Nicola Salvi, the waterfalls and pools are created with hydraulic engineering.

illusionary marvel: Hydraulic engineering creates its waterfalls and pools. Like the earlier creations of Bernini, Salvi's Fountain of Trevi affects multiple senses. It is an extravagant playground for sunlight and rushing water, for the grandeur of architecture and the grace of sculpture. Like modern theater, the monument invites interaction between itself and the spectator.

St. Paul's Cathedral

The baroque style caught on slowly in England. Unlike other European rulers, British monarchs, uneasy with the new parliamentary system of government, tried not to openly advertise their wealth for fear of making themselves unpopular. One of England's greatest architects, however, was very fond of baroque. In the mid-seventeenth century, Christopher Wren had the chance to use the style in a way uniquely his own. Wren's imagination left its mark not only in England but on buildings going up in the New World of North America.

A disaster gave Wren the opportunity to show his genius. In 1666 flames destroyed most of London, and after the Great Fire, King Charles II asked Wren to redesign the city. The project included rebuilding dozens of churches, including St. Paul's Cathedral.

St. Paul's, the largest church in England, is Christopher Wren's masterpiece. His reconstruction lasted from 1675 until 1709. Before he could begin, however, he had to tone down his enthusiasm for baroque forms to please the king and his advisers. The clergy who would be using the new St. Paul's had insisted on a tradi-

Architecture as a Stage Set

In her book People and Spaces, *writer Anita Abramovitz explains the Renaissance era's preoccupation with the theater and tells how it is reflected in the drama and artifice of its architecture. The theatrical element in architecture carried over into the baroque period as well.*

"Theater is a good example of what is meant by the illusionary possibilities of perspective. We already know that in ancient Greece the theater was outdoors, built into or carved out of an undulating, hilly natural arena space, and that in Roman days the theater moved indoors, developed structured tiers of seats, the curtain, and a fairly impressive stage with niches and statuary. This gave a backdrop with an impression of scenery, but in the Renaissance the modern illusionary effect of three-dimensional scenery began to develop. Lanes cut through the stage backdrop were narrowed from front to back to give the illusion of roads, and all the effects of sky, horizon, buildings, and depth, so familiar today, were begun at this time.

More important, what was happening on stage in experiments with perspective was the same sort of experimentation that was going on in the design of facades and interiors of buildings. Effects were achieved by using all kinds of decorative elements—columns, cornices, balustrades, paintings, carving, and sculpture.

Exteriors, too, were planned to reflect a plan in perspective: courts, squares, stairways, walks, buildings, wherever possible, were designed as a composition in a setting. Shakespeare, who wrote, 'All the world's a stage . . .' during Renaissance years, anticipated the baroque landscape of the seventeenth and eighteenth centuries perfectly. The city planning was, above all, a dramatic and three-dimensional theatrical setting, creating living backdrops for royal elegance and church panoply."

tional, cathedral-like look, rejecting Wren's first plans because they contained too many baroque elements, such as a domed entrance hall and a classical-style porch. The original St. Paul's had been Gothic, with the usual long nave, side aisles, and transept. Wren agreed to this format, then used his knowledge of Renaissance architecture to bring together several different elements in harmony.

Architect Christopher Wren combined the styles of many past architects when he redesigned St. Paul's cathedral in England. The dome is imitative of St. Peter's; the octagonal base was modeled after Bramante's Tempietto.

Inspired by St. Peter's, Wren designed a high dome for St. Paul's, topped with a columned cupola. The dome crowned an octagonal base ringed with columns, which Wren modeled after Bramante's Tempietto. The dome is framed by two towers whose tops are also surrounded by columns. The tall front wall carries two tiers of paired columns. Here Wren deliberately imitated the east facade of the palace of the Louvre, a French baroque building with a classic feel. St. Paul's Cathedral is Renaissance in feeling. But the combination of classic forms borrowed from different sources with a Gothic floor plan creates a stylish mixture that is indeed baroque.

Wren was not able to carry out his assignment to rebuild the city of London, however. His overall plan would have done away with old property lines; irate real estate special interest groups pressured King Charles into rejecting the architect's project. Wren was still in demand nevertheless, and he drew up plans for the rebuilding of forty-five small churches, leaving his unique stamp on each of them. Although many of the parishioners he worked with dreamed of Gothic spires, Wren wanted to work in a more modern, baroque style. He compromised by topping each church with a distinctive steeple. A Wren steeple usually began as a multisided tower that rose into a base decorated with classical columns. This stage was topped by a circular or octagonal platform for the steeple itself.

Wren's influence was far-reaching. English architects copied his trademark steeples, continuing to build them after his death in 1723. And his churches influenced the churches and public buildings of the new colonies in North America. In fact, the U.S. Capitol in Washington, D.C., is patterned after St. Paul's Cathedral.

The baroque style, then, was an outgrowth of the increasing power of royalty in the seventeenth and eighteenth centuries. Monarchs competed to exhibit their splendor by commissioning great city squares, palaces, monuments, and public buildings. Both the Renaissance and baroque styles formed architectural "stage sets" for royal performances. However, while the play was going on, the audience of common people was starving.

Europe and the American colonies were undergoing major changes. By the middle of the eighteenth century, democracy was a new hope glistening on the horizon. In 1776 the thirteen colonies won a war of independence. The bloody French Revolution followed in 1789. The glory days of monarchy were over forever. Along with revolution came an about-face in architectural styles. Anything that catered to the rich or celebrated financial excess at the expense of the poor was instantly unpopular. Baroque architecture, characterized by extreme, overblown decoration, was one such casualty. An architecture more suited to the modern age would follow on its heels.

Even though Renaissance structures were designed and created during a time of privilege, comfort, and financial plenty for the ruling class, the Renaissance itself generated today's beliefs in the importance of justice, equality, and the individual. By the eighteenth century, political upheaval and the coming Industrial Revolution brought the common people to center stage, with the result that the luxurious Renaissance and baroque styles, which represented the elite, were no longer fashionable. But the influence of these styles lingers in many European and American buildings. According to Victoria Kloss Ball:

> Italy in the fifteenth and sixteenth centuries began the art world's trek into today. Society turned its back on the feudal political system and on the solely religious philosophy of the Middle Ages. It turned toward capitalism and toward a rationally organized mode of thought. Stimulated by broadened horizons, artistic creativity burgeoned.[40]

5 The Eighteenth and Nineteenth Centuries

Two new architectural styles emerged: historicism and romanticism. Historicism, the recreation of old building styles, had been used by the ancient Romans, and during the Romanesque, Renaissance, and baroque periods. But more modern architects had scholarship as well as sentiment to empower their reworkings of old designs. For the first time, architects began to research old styles scientifically. In the mid-eighteenth century, the discovery of the buried cities of Pompeii and Herculaneum revealed what ancient Roman architecture had really looked like. These startling images of the past became models for historicist architects. These "architect-scholars" not only recaptured the past in their work, but used their knowledge to create new designs. Historicism was not just a hodgepodge drawn from different eras. It was an imaginative new movement that suited the changing society it served.

The second style, romanticism, was related to historicism. The eighteenth century, known as the Age of Reason, valued intellectual thought; but the Renaissance idea of the value of the individual had

The rediscovery of the ancient city of Pompeii heavily influenced architects in the mid-eighteenth century.

given birth to a new appreciation of feelings and emotions. The eighteenth century thus also became the Age of Sensibility, or feeling. Those who tended to emphasize feelings over reason started the romantic movement, which was characterized by a rebellious dissatisfaction with the way society operated. Romantics believed in breaking rules and following dreams. They wanted either to overthrow everything and start over or to escape into a fantasy world of distant times and places. Both romantic impulses—to build a future and to escape to the past—found inspiration in the forms proposed by historicist architecture. The new architecture offered structures that embodied ancient values in radical new arrangements.

New Engineering Technology

In the nineteenth century, scientific advances suddenly gave architects the chance to work with new materials as well as the traditional wood and stone. In addition, improvements in metallurgy, the science of separating metals from their ores, lowered the price of iron. Thus iron was no longer confined to a role in decoration. Nineteenth-century architects began to experiment with its advantages and disadvantages as a building material. Another new material, modern concrete, came into favor with architects more slowly than metal. Concrete is made of sand, broken stone, water, and cement. Portland cement, an artificial cement invented in 1824 by an English bricklayer, became popular, but it is weak under stress. To overcome this disadvantage, builders learned to reinforce concrete with embedded iron bars, a system originating in England in 1854. Iron and reinforced concrete became the building blocks of a new breed of architecture, the ancestor of the modern skyscraper. The experimental, and often strange-looking, buildings and structures made from the new materials both shocked and delighted the public.

The Gothic Revival

One of the most imaginative and, to our modern-day eyes, amusing movements of the eighteenth century was the Gothic revival in England. Technically, Gothic architecture did not need to be revived, since English towns and countrysides were scattered with churches, houses, and other buildings dating back to the Middle Ages. But England was just becoming conscious of its medieval heritage. Scholars began researching the origins of the country's accumulations of Gothic structures. Many of these researchers were emotionally drawn to the subject. The poet Thomas Warton loved to gaze on Gothic ruins by moonlight. In 1763 he published a sketchbook showing his ideas about the style's origin and development. But it was not until the mid-nineteenth century that historical knowledge about Gothic architecture became accurate. For example, the English were surprised to learn that the French, not the Goths, had invented the Gothic style.

Meanwhile, elements of moodiness associated with the Gothic style had captured the English public's imagination— the contemporary emphasis on feelings popularized any style that prompted an emotional reaction. In its eighteenth-century audience, therefore, the Gothic style provoked melancholy, dread, and even horror. This mock terror was entertaining, just as horror movies are today. Then a stream of so-called Gothic novels began to roll off the presses, melodramatic tales of gloom and doom in remote, mysterious settings. One novel, published in 1764, started the whole trend: *The Castle of Otranto: A Gothic Story*, by Horace Walpole. Filled with passion and horror, the tale was set in a haunted castle. The literary trend reached its height with the publication of Victor Hugo's famous novel, *Notre-Dame de Paris*, with its memorable hunchback, Quasimodo.

Literature influenced architecture in the eighteenth century. The highly popular Gothic novel gave way to a renewed interest in Gothic architecture. Horace Walpole, a writer of Gothic romances, designed his home, Strawberry Hill, to imitate Gothic designs.

Strawberry Hill

Horace Walpole, the author of *Otranto*, was responsible for starting the Gothic revival in architecture. On his retirement in 1748, he bought a small home called Strawberry Hill, overlooking the Thames River. In consultation with friends who shared his hobby of architectural dabbling, he created a Gothic dream house. Each room was lavishly decorated in authentic Gothic style. A wall screen in one room was a copy of a medieval gate in Rouen, the city where Joan of Arc was burned at the stake; the room's fireplace was based on a tomb in Canterbury Cathedral, the see (seat) of the head of the Church of England. The library, decorated with rows of pointed arches, was patterned after engravings of Old St. Paul's Cathedral. The effect was charming, but spooky.

Fonthill Abbey

The quaint Strawberry Hill found a critic in Horace Walpole's archenemy, millionaire William Beckford, who derided the house as a "Gothic mousetrap." He set out to outdo Walpole by building a Gothic mansion of his own, which he called Fonthill Abbey (1795–1807). For the ambitious project, Beckford hired James Wyatt, the greatest Gothic revival architect of the period.

Beckford's original concept was to have Wyatt build a replica of an abbey, or monastery, in ruins. Beckford wanted only one or two rooms suitable for living in, so that he could retreat there to brood in solitude. But the architect and his client soon decided to build a complete structure, a full-scale version of a Gothic cathe-

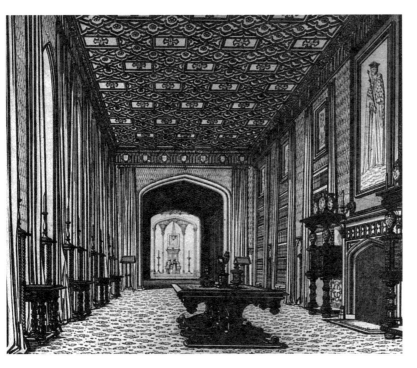

Millionaire William Beckford wanted to outdo Horace Walpole's Strawberry Hill when he designed and built his home, Fonthill Abbey. Beckford originally wanted the building to resemble a ruin, but the architect refused.

dral, with a 276-foot spiked tower and an echoing interior of tunnel-like corridors. Beckwith's domestic retreat was a cavernous cathedral rivaling in its delicious gloom and terror the haunted castle Otranto of his rival Walpole's novel. Ironically, because the building contractors had cheated Beckwith in constructing the foundation for the tower, the looming structure collapsed in 1825, tearing down most of the building as it fell. Beckwith then had the ruined Gothic abbey he had originally wanted.

The Picturesque Style

The picturesque style was an offshoot of the historic and romantic movements. Architects who pursued the picturesque mixed styles from different time periods, intentionally achieving a look of irregularity. These constructions were designed to blend in artistically with their natural surroundings. In the mid-eighteenth century, the English architect John Wood the Younger used the picturesque style to create a new concept in city planning.

Bath Circus and the Royal Crescent

John Wood's father was responsible for redeveloping the English country town of Bath, which had become fashionable for its healthy springs. To cash in on the trend, landowners were building row houses, similar to condominiums, in the area, which had been settled by the Romans in the first century A.D. John Wood the Elder decided to bring Bath's ancient history into the present day by recreating some of its old Roman monuments. His

Assigned to rebuild the ancient town of Bath, John Wood decided to recreate buildings to honor the town's Roman ancestry. Here is seen the Royal Crescent, a neighborhood of thirty houses.

most successful replica was the Bath Circus, from the Latin word for circle. Essentially, Wood turned the design of the Roman Coliseum, a stadium, inside out. He arranged thirty-three houses to face a central circular green crossed by three streets. The buildings were fronted by rows of double columns. John Wood the Younger topped his father's success in 1767 by designing a neighborhood of thirty houses at the end of one of the three streets of Bath Circus. Like an outstretched arm, the houses of the Royal Crescent march in a grand curve, fronted by a massive facade of Ionic columns that makes them appear to be joined into one unit. Their graceful procession overlooks a wide, sloping lawn. The picturesque city development at Bath used bits and pieces of Roman architecture and coordinated them with the flavor and history of the countryside in a way that charmed viewers.

Regent's Park

Regent's Park in London, the greatest example of English city planning, was inspired in the mind of John Nash by the Bath development. Nash was a well-respected architect and leader of the picturesque movement who had already designed an amazing town, called Blaise Hamlet (1811), of thatched and dormered country cottages patterned after those in old villages. In 1815 he remodeled the Royal Pavilion in Brighton in a bold, fantastic mix of Gothic, Chinese, and Indian elements, using domes and minarets to give the building the dreamlike, exotic look of an Arabian Nights palace.

Between 1812 and 1817, given the go-ahead by his patron, King George IV, Nash designed his most important project, a development in a spacious neighborhood in the heart of London. Nash in-

English architect John Nash designed many buildings in London, including the Royal Pavilion (right), and Regent's Park (below).

tended Regent's Park to include about fifty houses, a lake, a royal vacation palace, and a church. Meandering down the middle was Regent Street, which ran from the park to Carlton House. Behind the park, Nash planned clusters of cottages for city dwellers. More than a neighborhood, Regent's Park was meant to be a self-sufficient city within a city, complete with its own services and markets. Ultimately, few of the houses and cottages Nash had planned were actually built. However, much of Regent's Park and Regent Street did make it past the blueprint stage, and

the area still forms a charming escape from city strife today. In keeping with the picturesque tradition, Regent's Park is a man-made construction that blends harmoniously with its natural setting.

Thomas Jefferson

Thomas Jefferson, the third president of the United States, was also an amateur architect under historicist influence. After a long stay in France, Jefferson returned to

Thomas Jefferson continued to work on his home, Monticello, until his death. He attempted to imitate many of the classic architectural designs he had seen in France.

Virginia smitten with the classical Roman architecture he had seen abroad. He found the architecture of the American colonies crude and boxy by comparison. In 1770 Jefferson designed and built his own residence, Monticello, which he is said to have called his "essay in architecture." He wanted it to reflect authentic classical forms. He kept revising it until his death. Jefferson found his inspiration in the work of a well-known sixteenth-century architect, Andrea Palladio, whose own work was inspired by classical Roman buildings. According to *Thomas Jefferson's University:*

> In Jefferson's day, architectural ideas were spread via published collections of domestic and public designs, called pattern books. Jefferson never traveled to the countryside near Venice where Palladio's villas, palazzos, and churches are scattered. Rather he knew Palladio's work through the pages of his pattern book, the *Four Books of Architecture*, which Jefferson considered an architectural "Bible."[41]

Jefferson also called on classical inspiration in designing the Virginia State Capitol at Richmond (1785–1798). He decided to model it after the Maison Carrée, a Roman-style temple he had admired in France. Since the building was to be a capitol, not a temple, some tinkering with the original plan was needed. For example, Jefferson had to add windows to the design. And limitations in local craftsmanship led him to choose the simple Ionic column order over the Maison Carrée's Corinthian columns.

Jefferson completed his second presidential term in 1809, then retired to work on what he is said to have called "the hobby of my old age," the campus of the University of Virginia at Charlottesville. Jefferson wanted to create a campus that would compete with the established northeastern universities and provide inspiration to faculty and students. Picturesque and charming, the original university layout consists of two rows of five pavilions, or small houses, connected by rows of columns. The ten pavilions face each other across a lawn that sweeps up to the main building, called the Rotunda, modeled after the Roman Pantheon with its circular walls and round dome. Jefferson called this arrangement an "academical village."

The "Academical Village"

Thomas Jefferson's plans for an "academical village" were long in the making and carefully devised, according to this account in Thomas Jefferson's University, *which also mentions the campus's most famous nineteenth-century resident.*

"Jefferson's design for the University of Virginia was unlike that of any American or European school. . . . As early as 1805, he wrote that a university 'should not be a house but a village.' His advice to the trustees of East Tennessee College five years later shows the evolution of the plan he would eventually use for the University [of Virginia], with its central lawn and professors' pavilions connected by student rooms and covered walkways. . . .

Each of the academical village's ten pavilions was based on a different classical model. Jefferson placed traditional temple-front pavilions close to the Rotunda and less conventional ones at the Lawn's far end. To make the pavilions appear equidistant from the perspective of the Rotunda steps, the distance between pavilions increases with their distance from the rotunda. . . .

Jefferson intended the first floor of each pavilion to be used for classrooms and offices. Instructors and their families lived rent-free on the second floor where balconies and walkways allowed them to stroll and visit other pavilion residents without encountering students. . . .

In 1819, Jefferson designed the Ranges, two parallel rows of student rooms east and west of the pavilions. In his initial plan, they faced the backs of the pavilions. On the advice of others he turned the Ranges away from the pavilions and added gardens between. This arrangement increased the faculty's privacy and reduced the potential for noisy exchanges between students. . . .

One of the University's best-known students lived briefly at 13 West Range. Edgar Allan Poe attended classes for one session in 1826, before gambling debts forced him to leave. His room appears as it might have in the 1820s, with typical period furnishings and a bed Poe is said to have owned."

Jefferson's other major architectural project was the University of Virginia. Jefferson designed the Rotunda to duplicate the Pantheon, only at half of the original building's size.

The pavilions were intended as rent-free homes for professors, who were to live in the upper story and conduct classes on the ground floor. The pavilions were modeled after various Roman buildings, and each was slightly different from every other. Jefferson intended the pavilions to serve as examples of architecture for students to study.

Jefferson designed the Rotunda, which he meant to house a library, at half the size of the Pantheon. As with the Virginia State Capitol, he had to add windows to the original model. On the Rotunda's lower levels, hourglass-shaped halls separated three oval rooms. Above, the domed ceiling arched across the library. According to *Thomas Jefferson's University*, the designer originally had big plans for this ceiling:

> Because of his interest in scientific observation and experimentation, Jefferson intended a planetarium for the library's dome. The concave ceiling was to be "painted sky-blue and spangled

with gilt stars" which an operator could position to reflect the appearance of the night sky. Jefferson even drew and described the "machinery for moving the operator," but the imaginative project was never carried out.[42]

In response to increasing enrollment, an additional building was added to the Rotunda's north side in 1853. In 1895 it caught fire. In a frantic effort to save the Rotunda, an engineering professor tried to separate it from the burning structure with dynamite. Unfortunately, the explosion set the wooden dome ablaze. Students rescued a few library books and dragged the statue of Jefferson from the flames on a mattress, but much of the exterior was destroyed. The leading architect of the day, Stanford White, was hired to rebuild the Rotunda. In the 1970s, the interior was restored to Jefferson's original design, and the University of Virginia received professional honors as an outstanding achievement in American architecture.

Thomas Jefferson was one of the first architects to go beyond merely borrowing elements of a past style; rather, he adapted specific buildings in a chosen style to new purposes.

Art Nouveau Architecture

Like the picturesque and other romantic architectural movements, the art nouveau style was a rejection of the historicism favored by traditionalists like Thomas Jefferson. Art nouveau (French for "new art") flourished briefly and brightly in Europe between 1890 and 1910. Sculptors and painters as well as architects expressed their individuality through the sumptuous new style, which was rich with curved, swirling lines and sensuous textures.

Hector Guimard

Parisian architect Hector Guimard is noted for his involvement in the intricate details of each facet of his buildings, from built-in furniture to door handles. Many details, including entrance gates, were of wrought iron. Guimard studied iron fabrication techniques at iron foundries to learn how to bend and shape the metal into fanciful, energetic, curving shapes that expressed his unique vision.

In 1900 Guimard used exciting curves with dramatic effect in his series of entrances for the Paris Métro, the local subway system. Nearly every Parisian became familiar with Guimard's work through his fantastic parade of over 140 art nouveau doorways, more than 90 of which still exist today. The parts to the doorways are interchangeable—early examples of prefabrication.

The sturdy but graceful doorways are typical of art nouveau in that they imitate natural forms: their archways resemble plant stalks rising delicately from the stone curb, topped by bud-shaped amber glass lanterns. The curving iron railings and the fan-shaped skylights resemble petals. The interior walls of the subway station entrances were often lined with orange-tinted porcelain enamel, suggesting the inside of a blossom. Guimard's Métro entrances were works of art, fashioned in the new architectural media of iron and glass. Even though they were lovely and decorative, their form served its useful purpose of guiding passengers to subway entrances and provided shelter from the weather. Their familiarity on Paris streets brought art nouveau architecture to the attention of the common public.

Antonio Gaudí

Spanish architect Antonio Gaudí was a true maverick. Writer George Barford

Parisian architect Hector Guimard designed the entrances to the Paris Métro in 1900 in the Art Nouveau style.

calls him one of the great twentieth-century architects. His curving, decorative forms classify him as part of the art nouveau movement, but his ingenious structural systems and imaginative choice of materials make him an original. His attention-getting buildings flowed, sometimes undulating like snakes, imparting a sense of motion that gave them vitality and force. He was skilled in engineering, as well as being an imaginative designer, so his unusual structures were strong and practical.

In 1887 Gaudí's patron, a nobleman named Eusebio Güell, commissioned designs for two pavilions—a gatekeeper's lodge and a stable—for his country estate in Barcelona. For the pavilion walls, Gaudí combined brick and tile with unglazed ceramic castings in abstract forms. These ceramic forms were to become a trademark of Gaudí's work. The project's most famous feature is the wrought iron gate connecting the two buildings. Using the sweeping curves of the art nouveau style, Gaudí adorned the gate with a striking wrought iron dragon, with spreading wings and a spiraling tail. The gate was known as Dragon Gate, and dragons became a favorite motif in Gaudí's work.

A second project Gaudí completed for Güell during this period brought the architect's charming vision to the public. Güell wanted to create a residential park on a hill north of Barcelona, the first park of its kind in Spain. Gaudí's enthusiasm for the project is apparent in its inventive design. In Güell Park he provided covered walkways for strolling pedestrians. Their tops were roadways for carriages and motorcars. More of Gaudí's famous ironwork gates proclaimed the park's entrance. Within the entrance court, Gaudí placed fountains ornamented with images of dragons and lizards. A covered open space supported by columns was roofed by a children's play area. This elevated playground was surrounded, not by a wall, but by a gorgeous undulating stone bench. The sloping, curving surfaces of the bench were covered with an assortment of bright tiles, some made from broken

Rebel architect Antonio Gaudí designed this wrought iron gate to include an enormous dragon. The dragon became a favorite element in many of Gaudí's designs.

Antonio Gaudí designed Güell Park, the first residential park in Spain. It included covered walkways for pedestrians. Above the walkways were paths for automobiles and carriages.

dishes. Güell Park is a unique fantasyland of nontraditional textures, shapes, and colors. It delights the senses, truly fitting the purpose of a public park.

Two apartment buildings on the fashionable Paseo de Gracia in Barcelona are among Antonio Gaudí's finest and most well known works. They resemble no other building style. The Casa Batlló (1905–1907) has a rippling facade. The rounded stonework is supported by slender, elongated stone columns that inspired the apartment building's nickname, "House of Bones." The upper windows of the facade are set like eyes within sockets beneath a startling curved roof ridge. Blue tile accents the unusual structure both inside and out.

A few blocks away stands the even more unusual Casa Mila apartment building, completed in 1910. The tall stone structure dominated the street, a huge, wavelike mass that citizens call the Stone Quarry because it resembles a natural stone cliff. Each rippling story is accented by freeform ornamental iron railings. Even the roof undulates, as it curves to conform to the curves of the structure. The roof is dotted with eccentric chimneys and towers with tops that resemble human faces. Two fifteen-foot-high glass entrance doors ribbed in looping ironwork connect the otherworldly structure to the ordinary street blow.

The free-form, airy, playful spirit of art nouveau was a reaction against tradition. Architects soon reacted against art nouveau, abandoning it in favor of a more streamlined look. In the 1950s, however, the style experienced a revival, fueled by the desire of many to express a rejection of rigidity and to celebrate harmony with the environment. The appeal of these concepts influenced the postmodernist movement of the late twentieth century.

The Casa Mila apartment building in Spain was completed in 1910. Gaudí designed it to resemble a natural stone cliff.

Experiments in Engineering

The Industrial Revolution changed the look of architecture forever. Churches, palaces, and public buildings were considered art, and architects continued to design them. But for the multitude of factories, bridges, railroad stations, warehouses, and worker housing that went up seemingly overnight, big business called on the engineer for help. Thus many structures that defined the face of the modern city were products of engineering, not necessarily of artistry. That is, they were practical but not always beautiful. However, as architects began to experiment with the new medium of cast iron, and later, steel, many came up with creations that are miracles of art and engineering combined.

The nineteenth century has been called the "Cast Iron Age." Cast iron was produced in mass quantities in the early and mid-nineteenth century in response to rising demand and easier methods of production and transportation. According to Trachtenberg and Hyman:

> In the case of cast iron, it is not an exaggeration to say that the early nineteenth century fell in love with the substance (believed God-given, being so useful and plentiful) and used it for everything imaginable. Bridges, conservatories, factories, commercial buildings, markets, museums, churches, and libraries in which cast iron was used (often in combination with glass now available in unlimited quantities) proliferated in the first half of the century.[43]

In the late nineteenth century, however, people discovered that exposed cast iron caught fire easily. Thus cast iron was replaced with steel, a purer form of iron that had been fireproofed. This was another step into the future, toward the birth of that twentieth-century phenomenon, the skyscraper.

The Crystal Palace

Before the skyscraper made its debut, architects worked wonders with glass and iron. Although damaged by fire in 1936 and demolished during World War II, London's Crystal Palace (1851) was an unforgettable structure, an amazingly light and airy construction of intersecting columns, girders, and trusses bolted together into a framework resembling an enormous web.

The Crystal Palace was erected as the main exhibition hall for London's Exposition of 1851, titled "The Great Exhibition of the Works of All Nations." Its designer, the talented architect and landscape artist Joseph Paxton, fashioned the Crystal Palace in the form of a giant greenhouse. The building was the largest in the world to that date: 70 feet tall, 408 feet wide, and 1,851 feet long. Like the Gothic cathedrals before and the skyscrapers to follow, its form was organic, similar to the human body, consisting of a skeleton of iron sheathed in a skin of glass. Anita Abramovitz writes of the structure:

> Paxton was able to create for the Exhibition a long, spacious, glass-and-iron prefabricated structure which from an engineering point of view would have been a singular technical achievement even as a factory building, yet to the amazement and delight of the thousands who eventually visited there, it

London's Crystal Palace was a network of glass and iron. Designed by Joseph Paxton, Victorians loved the building, which seemed to portend great things for the future.

retained the ambience and charm of garden greenhouses and orangeries.[44]

People fell in love with the spectacular building, put at ease by its familiar layout. Like an English cathedral, the Crystal Palace had a long, multi-aisled interior crossed by a high, barrel-vaulted transept enclosing a huge, live tree. The Crystal Palace evoked the future, its walls and ceiling seeming to magically disintegrate into thin air. The repeated segments of its prefabricated iron web retreated into the distance as dazzled visitors peered down the building's seemingly limitless length. The entire interior of the transparent structure was fancifully painted in alternating bands of red, yellow, and blue on white.

The Brooklyn Bridge

New York's Brooklyn Bridge (1867–1883) is a triumph of art as well as engineering. One of the first bridges to employ the new material of steel, it also uses the ancient medium of stone, combining history with science. Designed by John Roebling, the Brooklyn Bridge is a suspension bridge; that is, its roadway hangs from steel suspension cables. In the Brooklyn Bridge, which links the southwestern tip of Long Island to the island of Manhattan, these wirelike cables are attached to massive stone towers. To support the heavy roadway, two systems of cables join forces. Vertical cables hang from the drooping curves that loop from tower to tower. In addition, crisscrossing cables stretch from the towers to regularly spaced spots on the roadway. The roadway itself was divided into two outside lanes for carriages, two inside lanes for a cable train, and an elevated central boardwalk for pedestrians.

The Brooklyn Bridge was a great success with the public. People saw it metaphorically, as a span representing the United States as a whole reaching out to the world, as well as to the future. However, art historians are often critical of the

The Brooklyn Bridge was one of the first bridges to use steel. The bridge's stone towers resemble Gothic architecture. The Statue of Liberty (right) was designed by Gustave Eiffel, the same man who designed the Eiffel Tower in Paris.

old-fashioned look of the stone towers, or piers, holding up the bridge. Roebling designed them to resemble the buttress towers on a Gothic cathedral. He also gave the tops of the piers an Egyptian flavor. The arches within the piers, while pointed, call Roman arches to mind. Critics feel that Roebling should have left out the mishmash of historic detail and designed streamlined, modern-looking piers. In fact, the Brooklyn Bridge's successful mixture of old and new styles makes it an ideal example of the melding of history and technology that characterized nineteenth-century architecture.

The Statue of Liberty

The greatest sculptural monument of the nineteenth century, the Statue of Liberty (1875–1886) still stands watch above New York Harbor, a testimony not only to freedom, but to the new technology that created the statue itself. Designed by the great French engineer Gustave Eiffel, who also designed the Eiffel Tower, the Statue of Liberty completely hides its modern inner structure of concrete and wrought iron within a hammered copper shell. To the casual observer, the statue is remarkable for its size: a three-hundred-foot-tall woman wears a crown and holds a torch skyward. The statue does not seem particularly modern. The copper figure on its granite base has a classical style, in fact.

Contrary to appearance, however, the Statue of Liberty is distinctly modern on the inside. The concrete core of the granite base is reinforced by bars of steel and iron. Inside the statue is a rigid framework of wrought iron, massive in the middle and lightweight toward the edges. This framework is attached to the interior "skin" of the statue with flexible iron bars that act like springs, bending in response to the statue's expansion and contraction with changing temperatures. The statue's copper shell merely hangs from this framework, as the walls of twentieth-century buildings would later dangle from steel supports.

The Eiffel Tower

Far from hiding its technology, Gustave Eiffel's famous tower shamelessly exposes its workings to all of Paris. While the tower has become the most familiar symbol of France, not everyone appreciated its shocking new look at the time. Eiffel erected his tower between 1887 and 1889 on the banks of the Seine River overlooking the entrance to a fairground. At three hundred meters tall (more than 980 feet), it could be seen from anywhere in the city. Many Parisian artists and writers were not

A Century of Rapid Change

The beginning and ending of the nineteenth century differed radically from each other, both socially and architecturally, according to Anita Abramovitz in People and Spaces.

"At the beginning of the 1800s life was lived at a rather leisurely pace. The stagecoach was the chief means of transportation by land; sailing ships commanded the seas. Local materials and regional crafts characterized almost all building. Before the end of the century steam was propelling hundreds of different machines, and European countries were producing such an excess of cheaply manufactured materials that new areas of the world were aggressively and frantically sought for colonization chiefly because, from an economic point of view, they were needed to provide not only raw materials but as return markets for surplus goods.

The century began, as far as architecture was concerned, with a continuation of the classic style and with the traditional aristocratic or court patron still in evidence as a client. It ended in a life style completely separated from the traditions of Renaissance Europe and in the disappearance of the noble patron and the appearance of a new client class oriented toward the economics of business. There came about a decline in the use of regional crafts, materials, and labor, but a great increase in the production of glass and metal, particularly iron and steel. The century began with Renaissance-Baroque techniques of construction and ended with the first scientifically planned foundation work for skyscrapers."

happy about that, calling the tower an insult to good taste because it did not resemble anything anyone had ever seen before.

The Eiffel Tower is made up of four tapering, curved piers rising from a square base. Each pier is latticed, or formed of crisscrossing metal pieces like lacework. The whole structure rises to a point, and its parts are firmly connected. The lightweight, spidery look alarmed Parisians, however, who feared the tower would topple over on them. In response to the public's worries, the architect added decorative ironwork in the form of arches at the base of the tower that made it visually appear to be more stable.

Trachtenberg and Hyman speculate that the established French culture may have objected to the Eiffel Tower on other grounds, as well. Standing high above all the existing buildings that represented the old way of thinking, the tower may have been perceived as a threat to those in power:

> Eiffel's tower rose impudently far above all the religious and dynastic buildings whose . . . styles had been adopted by the ruling bourgeoisie [middle-class commercial interests]; worse, its advanced system of elevators carried daily tens of thousands of ordinary working-class Parisians to a viewpoint high above everything. . . . Paris, so recently ravaged by socialist revolution, lay at their feet. . . . The Tower was the new iron "cathedral" of [the people] of nineteenth-century Paris.[45]

The eighteenth and nineteenth centuries straddled the threshold between the old world and the new. Eighteenth-century historicism and romanticism reached backward, plucking old architec-

The Eiffel Tower, which has become the most familiar landmark in France, was controversial and widely disliked by the French people.

tural elements from the mists of the past and reworking them into new, futuristic forms. The developing technology of the nineteenth century became an artistic medium for architects to play with, experimenting with new materials as well as new forms to create fantasy structures that paid a debt to the past while celebrating the future. Not until the twentieth century, however, would a new structural system, steel cantilever construction, usher in the architectural style known today as "modern."

6 Modern Architecture

In the twentieth century, factory workers replaced craftspeople. Trains and motorcars outdistanced stagecoaches and carriages. There were new modes of communication and modern concepts in medicine and education. After the Civil War, in the mid-nineteenth century, America experienced a population explosion in its cities. European immigrants and former residents of rural areas flooded urban centers to fill job openings in factories and offices. Land space was at a premium. A new building concept, the tall, vertical building or skyscraper, gave landlords the chance to multiply their rent by increasing the space available in their new buildings.

Thus, the skyscraper became the rage. According to writer James Cross Giblin, the word *skyscraper* was a borrowed term for the new preoccupation with tall buildings:

In the 19th century, [the word] was used for several other things that seemed to "scrape the sky." A skyscraper was the tallest sail on a clipper ship, and high bonnets and hats were also called skyscrapers. So was a baseball that was hit or thrown high into the air. The word was first applied to tall buildings in 1883, when the magazine *American Architect* published a letter saying, "America needs tall buildings; it needs skyscrapers."[46]

The Structure of a Skyscraper

In the early nineteenth century, architects experimented with tall buildings, but existing construction methods limited the height of these projects. Tall buildings made of stone had to have thick walls to support the weight of their upper stories. Architects tried to counteract the pressing weight by using iron frames to support the floors of tall buildings. But the stone or brick walls still had to bear their own weight. In the 1880s, however, architects realized that they could use steel frames to support their buildings' walls, as well as just the floors.

Besides allowing for added height, steel frames offered many advantages that influenced the design of subsequent tall buildings. A steel frame lifted the burden of support from the walls, allowing them to become thinner. Thinner walls, in turn, allowed more room for shop or office space on each floor. In addition, rooms could have more light because thin walls

Elevators and Skyscrapers

The towering skyscraper would not have been practical without the new technology of the elevator. In The Skyscraper Book, *James Cross Giblin describes a dramatic demonstration by one of its inventors.*

"The inventor Elisha Otis created a sensation when he demonstrated a steam-powered elevator at [an exhibition] in New York in 1853. Accompanied by an assistant, Otis mounted a platform in the central exhibition hall. As a large crowd watched, a cable hoisted the platform high into the air. Then the assistant handed Otis a dagger on a velvet cushion. The crowd gasped and drew back as Otis began to cut through the cable with a dagger. The last fibers separated—but nothing happened; invisible safety catches were holding up the platform. The crowd applauded as Otis descended safely to the floor.

After the exhibition, Otis patented his invention and established a factory to manufacture passenger elevators. In the 1870s, hydraulic elevators operated by water or oil pressure replaced the less efficient steam-powered models. By the late 1880s, lighter and faster electric elevators began to come into use, just when they were needed for the new skyscrapers that were being planned."

could accommodate more windows. Finally, a steel frame building was cheaper to build, since it could be erected more quickly than a stone one.

By the twentieth century, architects had begun to incorporate a revolutionary new method in the design of their steel frame buildings: cantilever construction. Art historians consider the discovery of cantilever construction to be as important as the discovery of the arch. A cantilever is a beam supported at only one end, something like a diving board. The beam is balanced so that it can carry an even load of weight all along its length. Nineteenth-century architects were familiar with the cantilever, but the technique of using it could not be perfected until the invention of tough, industrial-strength steel.

Cantilevered beams could be used to create an internal steel skeleton for a building. Steel uprights provide the main support, with horizontal beams cantilevering outward from the center. Floors rest on these beams, similar to stacked trays. As for the walls, instead of holding up the building, in a cantilevered structure walls literally hang from the beams, like curtains from rods. The walls thus became the skin clothing the steel skeleton. Since they did not bear weight, walls could be made almost entirely of glass, another material that could be cheaply manufactured by the twentieth century. The steel-and-glass skyscraper would not have been born without the perfection of cantilevered construction.

The Woolworth Building

Although Chicago was the actual birthplace of the skyscraper, it is New York City that seems synonymous with the structure. The Woolworth Building (1913), built to resemble a Gothic structure, is a good example of a modern building dressed in the costume of the past. It took a while for architects to begin designing buildings that complemented the nature of the modern materials they were using. For many decades, skyscrapers were still ornamented in classical detailing, making for an incongruous, tacked-on effect, as George Sullivan points out:

> Why . . . should an architect use a great Roman arch over a window or doorway when a simple steel or iron lintel would do? Why plaster Doric, Ionic, or Corinthian cast iron columns on building exteriors? What was the sense of baroque cornices, Roman pediments and Grecian entablatures as elements of design? These things had no meaning; they were mere "frosting."[47]

The Woolworth Building, designed by Cass Gilbert, is a high tower thrusting from a rectangular base. It is replete with Gothic ornamentation, including a pointed, Gothic "hat" perched on its top. However, its appearance is both striking and graceful, and its history makes it a worthy recipient of the honor of being named an official landmark of New York City.

The historic building was commissioned by Frank W. Woolworth, founder of the dime-store chain. Woolworth was a rags-to-riches millionaire who had started his working life as a store clerk. He wanted a building to match the magnificence of his millions. To satisfy Woolworth's admiration for Gothic architecture, Cass Gilbert designed a tower decorated with arches, spires, flying buttresses, and gargoyles (grotesque stone figures). But the building design also included modern lines in the strong piers that rise up from the main mass. The skyscraper cost $13.5 million to construct.

The Woolworth Building in New York City was built to resemble a Gothic building. One of the first skyscrapers ever built, it is considered an official landmark of New York City.

The Woolworth Building was built as an office building with many charming details, including gargoyles in the lobby that sport the faces of those who built the building.

Like most skyscrapers, the Woolworth Building was an office building, a monument to business enterprise. The Woolworth Building was described as a "cathedral of commerce," partly because its grand ground floor lobby resembles a Moorish palace or Gothic cathedral, with marbled walls, an arched ceiling decorated with colored mosaic tiles, and a majestic marble stairway. Tucked whimsically under the lobby ceiling beams are gargoyles representing not dragons or animals but real people involved in the building's construction. One of them is a caricature of Frank W. Woolworth, counting the nickels and dimes he amassed

from the public that made the building possible.

At sixty stories, the Woolworth Building was the tallest building in the world to that date. The structure could have accommodated more stories if the ceilings had been of average height, but Woolworth had insisted on high ceilings to match the overall Gothic flavor. Some of the ceilings rose to twenty feet. The building contains over five thousand windows. It was the first skyscraper to have its own power plant: four generators churn out enough electricity to supply a city of fifty thousand people.

To celebrate the completion of his monument to himself, Woolworth gave a fancy dinner party for over eight hundred guests on the building's twenty-seventh floor. At 7:30 P.M. all the lights in the banquet hall dimmed while a Western Union telegraph operator flashed a signal to the White House. President Woodrow Wilson responded by pressing a button that lit the towering structure with over eighty thousand electric bulbs, blazing against the night sky. For almost twenty years, the Woolworth Building reigned as the world's tallest building. Today, it is still among the tallest, and certainly ranks as one of the most beautiful and fanciful as well.

The Chrysler Building

Upon its completion in 1930, New York's Chrysler Building supplanted the Woolworth Building as the tallest building in the world. However, it did not hold that title long. Commissioned by the Chrysler Motors Corporation and designed by William Van Allen, the building's steel spire stretched to 1,048 feet. The Chrysler

Building is considered a striking example of the art deco style of architecture. Its stainless steel casing glistens in the sun. It tapers to an elegant point at the top, where six rows of curving metal arcs set with triangular windows come together in a peak like a bishop's miter. The building is just as delightful close up as it is at a distance: the high exterior walls are enlivened with bands of inlaid colored brick arranged to form portraits of the front ends of automobiles in profile, a comment on the building's origin. Automobile worship is further carried out in the gargoyles arranged around the upper story, which are modeled after car hood ornaments. According to Giblin: "More than almost any other skyscraper, the Chrysler Building reflected the energy, optimism, and zest for living that characterized the 1920s."[48] The building seems as modern now as the day it was built. Its sassy style appeals to the imagination: An animated version of the building found its way into a recent soft drink commercial.

The Empire State Building

Even as the Chrysler Building was opening, the foundations for the Empire State Building were being laid. Just as the Eiffel Tower symbolizes Paris, the Empire State Building (1931) symbolizes New York City. It also holds the record for being the fastest-rising skyscraper ever built. Designed by William F. Lamb, it was commissioned by a group of businessmen who all wanted the structure to go up quickly. This put pressure on Lamb to design it quickly, but he ultimately went through several revisions of his original plan. His first drawing is said to have been based on a distinctly ordinary object, a sharpened pencil stood on end.

Over eighty stories high, the building was budgeted at $60 million. More than three thousand bricklayers, carpenters, electricians, plumbers, elevator installers, and other workers swarmed over the construction site daily. To minimize time lost at lunch hour, mobile snack bars shuttled up and down the scaffolding. A small emergency hospital was housed in the basement of the building to contend with frequent accidents. The skyscraper's steel skeleton was completed in an amazing twenty-three weeks, but the speeded-up building schedule took the lives of four-

When it was completed in 1930, the Chrysler Building was taller than the Woolworth Building. Its familiar rows of arches at the top are classically art deco in style.

teen construction workers, who died from injuries incurred while rushing to complete the job.

Construction of the Empire State Building was finished ahead of schedule on April 11, 1931. The amazing new building contains seventy-three elevators whizzing through seven miles of shafts. Gigantic air conditioners replace stale air with fresh six times an hour. The structure has sixty-five hundred windows, each needing washing twice a month. For the grand opening, following the custom set by Woodrow Wilson for the Woolworth Building, President Herbert Hoover, in Washington, pushed the button that lit the Empire State Building's gorgeous marble lobby.

The public was duly impressed. Unfortunately, between the building's conception and its completion, an event began that distracted the public's attention, as well as its funds—the Great Depression.

Because of the poor economy, less than a third of the offices inside the Empire State Building were rented in 1931. This earned the skyscraper the nickname "Empty State Building." However, the flocks of sightseers who paid the large sum (in those days) of one dollar apiece to visit the building soon helped make up the difference. On the day it opened, five thousand people visited. In a month, a hundred thousand people had seen the skyscraper. Soon the world saw it via film when the building was featured in the classic movie *King Kong.*

Since its opening, the Empire State Building has withstood some shocks. In 1945 a B-25 bomber rammed into the north side of the building with a crash that sounded like an earthquake. The impact sheared off the army plane's wings, but it kept going, tearing a hole eighteen feet wide and twenty feet high in the wall of the skyscraper. The plane's gas tanks ex-

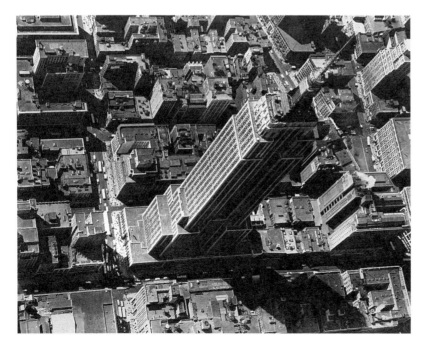

The Empire State Building is as much the quintessential landmark of New York City as the Eiffel Tower is of Paris. A B-25 bomber once crashed into the building.

Skyscrapers as Landing Strips

The top of the Empire State Building was originally intended to be a landing area for dirigibles, but the dangerous idea was soon abandoned, according to James Cross Giblin in The Skyscraper Book.

"From the observation deck [of the Empire State Building] the guests could look up at the 200-foot-high . . . mooring mast that had been placed at the very top of the building's tower.

The mast had been designed as a landing for dirigibles, the giant airships that were then the latest thing in air travel. If all had gone according to plan, transatlantic dirigibles would have flown up Manhattan Island and hooked onto the mooring mast atop the Empire State Building. An enclosed gangplank would have been lowered from the airship, and the passengers would have walked down it to a platform at the top of the building. From the platform express elevators would have whisked them down to the street.

Engineers warned that airships would swing too much in the wind for the mooring mast to work safely. But it was built in spite of the warnings. . . .

On September 15, 1931, a privately owned dirigible tied up to the mast, but stayed only three minutes because a 45-mile-an-hour . . . wind was whipping the airship. . . .

No passenger dirigible ever tied up to the mast, and dirigible travel itself went out of style after the German airship *Hindenburg* burst into flames, killing all on board, while attempting to land at Lakehurst, New Jersey, in 1937. Eventually the landing platform was transformed into a second, higher observation deck on what became the 102nd story of the Empire State Building."

ploded, igniting the building's seventy-eighth and seventy-ninth floors. The pilot, crew, and eleven office workers died. Fortunately, the crash occurred on a Saturday, sparing an untold number of lives.

The Empire State Building was involved in crashes of a different type that first occurred in large numbers during the sixties. Attracted by the bright floodlights on the top thirty floors of the building, birds migrating in the spring and fall began accidentally flying into the light and smashing themselves. This usually occurred during foggy nights when birds are most easily confused. Over four hundred birds crashed into the skyscraper on a single rainy night in 1970. After that, authorities stopped turning on the floodlights at night, a decision that has saved many birds.

Much U.S. history has been witnessed by America's most famous skyscraper. In 1979 it was declared an official New York City landmark. It has remained a well-loved American monument as well.

Rockefeller Center

One of the advantages of the "glass box" style made popular by skyscrapers is that walls consisting mostly of windows can let in maximum amounts of light for the people inside to enjoy. However, unless the buildings are set back—that is, unless their stories become progressively smaller as the building climbs higher—skyscrapers can spoil the view for surrounding buildings and for pedestrians, casting giant shadows across a city. And, if spaced too close together, they can spread shadows on one another. Early skyscrapers were intended to solve the problem of urban overcrowding. Instead, they threatened to overcrowd the cities themselves. James Cross Giblin discusses an early response to the problem:

> As more and more skyscrapers were built, more and more people crowded into city centers to work and to shop, and traffic became extremely congested.
>
> In 1923, Harvey Wiley Corbett, a professor of architecture at Columbia University, proposed a solution to the traffic problem in New York City. He suggested that pedestrians walk along second-story sidewalks, cantilevered out from the walls of tall buildings, and cross streets on bridges at the corners. Meanwhile, as many as 20 lanes of traffic would roar through the broad streets and avenues below.
>
> Corbett's suggestions were never followed, and people continued to build new skyscrapers, despite the problems they created.[49]

Others proposed a city within a city, in which workers lived in the same skyscrapers that housed their offices. Thus, commuter traffic and parking problems would be eliminated, as workers took elevators to work, and strolled to nearby shops and theaters, located in the same cluster of buildings. While this plan did not materialize either, the cluster idea was carried out on a small scale in the design of Rockefeller Center (1931–1940).

Rockefeller Center is a welcoming blend of shops, theaters, spacious courtyards, and soaring office towers in the heart of Manhattan. Designed by a team of architects including Raymond Hood, it was commissioned by John D. Rockefeller Jr. and his family. The center now includes eighteen buildings that cover twenty-two acres. A large sunken plaza includes a bronze statue of the Greek god Prometheus hovering above a marble fountain. Prometheus, who taught humans to use fire, was chosen to symbolize the theme of human progress that pervades the center. (Interestingly, murals painted by the renowned Mexican artist Diego Rivera were removed from the lobby of one of the buildings, since they represented political views distasteful to the wealthy client. In their place were installed three-dimensional portraits of fa-

Rockefeller Center plaza is a network of shops, theaters, and courtyards. At the center of a large sunken plaza rests a bronze statue of the Greek god Prometheus.

mous Americans such as Abraham Lincoln.)

An outdoor café and ice-skating rink are situated beside the Prometheus fountain. Every year, a giant Christmas tree is set up in the plaza overlooking the fountain. From the plaza, five sleek, gray skyscrapers dominate the view, ranging in height from the sixteen-story Eastern Airlines Building to the seventy-story RCA Building. Unlike earlier skyscrapers, these towers are free of decoration. Their bareness represents the trend that would characterize skyscrapers to follow: clean-cut, severe outlines and an avoidance of historical reference.

In 1969 this "skyscraper city" was honored with a citation from the American Institute of Architects. Giblin quotes some of the reasons given for the award:

To a lesson in land use which devotes such large areas to air and space, but also to human enjoyment. To a group of high structures which offered a new approach to urban planning. To a project so vital to the city and alive with its people that it remains as viable today as when it was built.[50]

Frank Lloyd Wright

The architect Frank Lloyd Wright was a maverick, a free-spirited individualist whose unique career spanned the first half of the twentieth century. While he designed tall buildings, he is most recognized for his use of long, low lines that hugged the landscape and for his simple, uncluttered interior spaces. His genius was recognized in Europe as well as in America—many architectural projects in the Netherlands show his influence.

According to legend, Wright's mother so wanted him to grow up to be an architect that she hung pictures of cathedrals above his crib. Wright ended up satisfying his mother's wish, but nevertheless he is known as a stubborn original thinker. He was a student of the successful architect Louis Sullivan, whose functional theory suggested that if an architect fully explored the problem to be solved by a building, the design arrived at would respond to the problem in a singularly appropriate way, untainted by historical influence. Each of Wright's buildings is a unique solution to a problem; no two approaches are exactly the same.

One of Wright's early successes was Chicago's Robie House (1909), designed for Frederick Carleton Robie. The low-

The Architect as Savior

In his autobiography, Testament, *Frank Lloyd Wright describes himself as a heretic for believing that architecture can liberate the individual human spirit.*

"I saw the architect as savior of the culture of modern American society; his services as the mainspring of any cultural life in America—savior now as for all civilizations heretofore. Architecture being inevitably the basis of an indigenous [native] culture, American architects must become emancipators of senselessly conforming human beings imposed upon by mediocrity and imposing mediocrity upon others in this sanitary but soulless machine-age. . . . Architecture of the machine-age should become not only fundamental to our culture but natural to the happiness of our lives in it as well. All this was rank heresy at the time. We have made some progress since because it does not seem so heretical now.

Young heretic, then, I freely spoke but steadily planned all the time. . . . I loved architecture as romantic and prophetic of a true way of life; life again coming beautifully alive today as before in the greatest ancient civilizations. We were free men now? The architect among us then should qualify as so inspired; be free leader of free human beings in our new free country. All buildings built should serve the liberation of mankind, liberating the lives of *individuals*. What amazing beauty would be ours if man's spirit, thus organic, should learn to characterize this new free life of ours in America as natural!"

In a sea of anonymity, architect Frank Lloyd Wright remains a well-known figure in modern architecture for his unique, easily recognizable designs.

The exterior of the Robie House, designed by Frank Lloyd Wright, features an overhanging roof designed to provide shade. Consistent with Wright's distaste for walls, the interior rooms of the house are uninterrupted by walls.

slung, three-story structure has a distinctive overhanging roof to shade it from the sun. It rests on a concrete slab, and its heating, electrical, and plumbing apparatus all cluster in a central core like a big fireplace hearth. Inside, walls and partitions are minimized, so that the viewers can see all the way through the house from one end to the other.

Wright called his fondness for removing walls "breaking the box." He used this technique on several houses he designed that came to be known as "prairie houses." Since only the bathrooms and bedrooms had walls, the homes were like vessels for flowing interior space. Wright's extensive use of windows makes the outside world appear to flow in, until the viewer is unsure about what is inside the house and what is outside. The prairie houses' horizontal lines echo the flat plains on which many of them were built.

Wright's later work was no less original. While he favored stone and wood over steel, he did not avoid modern materials. His Unity Church in Oak Park, Illinois (1937) shows one of architecture's first uses of rectangular and decorative forms appropriate to concrete. Wright's best loved design, popularly known as Fallingwater House (1937), built in Bear Run, Pennsylvania, was designed for the Pittsburgh millionaire Edgar J. Kaufmann. Like his prairie homes, Wright's design for Fallingwater responds to surroundings. A stream rushes alongside the house and cascades in a waterfall beneath it, forming an intimate connection between the building and its natural setting.

Fallingwater House (left) and the Guggenheim Museum (below) are two of Wright's most famous designs.

Wright was no stranger to controversy. His design for the Guggenheim Museum (1956–1959) was perhaps the most criticized of his career. The building's main exhibition hall is a huge spiral ramp, making the outside of the art museum resemble a giant snail. Pictures are hung on the ramp's outer walls, and museum-goers view them as they stroll downward through the spiraling passage. Wright wanted to heighten visitors' participation in the artistic event rather than constraining them to be passive observers, but many critics feel that the building's odd design distracts people from the artwork that is displayed.

Frank Lloyd Wright's brilliance lay in his ability to put modern technology to work in harmony with nature, rather than in opposition to it. The simple lines of his buildings were a break from the overblown ornamentation of the past. His projects were organic wholes, like living beings interacting with the outside world. Trachtenberg and Hyman comment on the architect's personality and influence:

Wright's uniquely flamboyant personality and sense of prophetic mission were . . . translated into his unique style, and developed as a personal cult among his students and public. He was the most futuristic of all the Modernists, especially in his early work, which leaped so far ahead of its time that it took the rest of the world nearly a generation to catch up.[51]

The International Style

According to art historians, the architectural movement known as the international style is the first truly original movement since the Gothic. The internationalists, beginning in the 1920s, took the new building materials and construction methods of steel, glass, concrete, and cantilever and worked them into a style all their own. The style stressed open interior spaces, light let in through glass walls, and stark outlines that had a machinelike precision. The style's critics found this deliberate severity too rigid and impersonal. Many later architects have reacted against the international style.

Walter Gropius

The German architect Walter Gropius was one of the founders of the international

Walter Gropius was one of the founders of the international style of architecture. This style was typified by the use of new twentieth-century building materials, such as steel, glass, and concrete.

style. Gropius was the head of an art school called the Bauhaus (architecture house) in Dessau, Germany. The Bauhaus stressed the impact of the machine on architecture. The architect's design for the workshop wing of the Bauhaus itself reflects the tenets of the international style. Built between 1925 and 1926, the Bauhaus appears to be a block of glass hovering in midair. Actually, the glass walls, which wrap around the entire structure, hang from a cantilevered roof. The concrete floors and columns inside the building can be seen through the glass. Followers of the international style did not believe in hiding any aspect of a building's framework.

Ludwig Mies van der Rohe

Ludwig Mies van der Rohe was a colleague of Walter Gropius. The architect, referred to as Mies, was one of the pioneers of the glass-sheathed skyscraper. He also favored the use of floor-to-ceiling glass wall panels for homes. The buildings Mies designed can be described as "skin and bones" architecture. Devoid of ornament, their lines are clean and pure. His motto is said to have been "Less is more."

Both Mies and Gropius escaped the Nazi regime during World War II and came to the United States, where their new style had an enormous impact on American architecture. In the later years of his influential career, Mies designed New York's 520-foot-high Seagram Building (1954–1958). The thirty-eight-story tower is clothed in solid bronze set with a closely spaced procession of tinted windows. The skyscraper is admired for its clean lines. From a distance, it appears to be a sleek, freestanding rectangle. Inside, the building is known for its sumptuous materials

Ludwig Mies van der Rohe designed the 520-foot Seagram Building. The much imitated building was one of the first to use the wall of glass that characterizes modern skyscrapers.

scrapers went up that the building type has fallen into disfavor.

Le Corbusier

Unlike Mies and Gropius, the Swiss architect Le Corbusier left his mark mainly on South American, Asian, and European cities. This is because his favorite medium was reinforced concrete, whereas steel was the preferred construction material in the United States. Le Corbusier, whose real name was Charles-Edouard Jeanneret, believed that a building's exterior should result from the purpose for which the building was to be used. Le Corbusier also had a fondness for basic forms, such as the cube, the cylinder, and the pyramid. The architect is famous for his belief that a house should be "a machine for living in."

In 1952 Le Corbusier built an apartment complex in Marseilles, France, that his critics called the Madman's House.

Swiss architect Le Corbusier designed Madman's House in 1952. Its boxy style, typical of twentieth century architecture, has become less admired today.

and careful detailing: walls are of travertine and pink granite, and the glass windows are tinted pinkish gray. Details such as elevator buttons, light fixtures, and door handles are crisply finished to complete the look of elegant simplicity.

Unfortunately, many lesser architects of the sixties and seventies imitated the stark, seemingly impersonal quality of the Seagram Building without giving their work the personal style of Ludwig Mies van der Rohe. So many "glass box" sky-

Le Corbusier's odd Chapel of Notre Dame du Haut in France is said to resemble a plow.

Taking five years to build at a cost of $6 million, it resembles a box on stilts. The box is honeycombed with 337 living units. The apartment complex embodies some of the dreams of international style followers in that it is meant to be a miniature city within a city. It contains its own interior street, as well as a lawn, a playground, a market, and a laundry. In some ways, it is similar to the planned communities being built today.

While some of Le Corbusier's designs were rectangular and boxy, some were based on curved lines, like his surreal Chapel of Notre Dame du Haut in Ronchamp, France (1955). This strange-looking church has a rough appearance that matches its country setting. The wedge-shaped building is topped with a heavy, flat roof whose edges curl up like a floppy hat brim. Its walls are slanted and set with small, irregularly spaced windows that look so casual that they appear to have just happened, rather than to have been placed there. The entire building is said to resemble a plow.

Gropius, Mies, and Le Corbusier, the three innovators of the international style, had many followers as well as many detractors. The debate about their stripped-down, functional design mode continued into the second half of the twentieth century.

Thus, in the twentieth century, social change resulting from the machine age and newly available building materials joined forces to stimulate architects to produce structures that, regardless of whether they were influenced by past styles, were distinctly modern. The last half of the twentieth century, however, would bring a rebellious rejection of modernism by cutting-edge architects, a movement called second modernism or postmodernism.

7 Contemporary Architecture

In the 1960s, a new wave swept over architecture, replacing the modernism of the international style and its followers. This new wave rejected modern architecture's severity and its avoidance of the past. Rather, it embraced the past, drawing on historical elements from different periods with self-conscious humor. The name of the movement itself was humorous and contradictory: postmodernism. Critics wondered how there could be anything more modern than modern architecture. Postmodernists began to demonstrate new possibilities, experimenting in a playful style that in addition to stealing ideas from history, made use of political symbolism, vivid decoration, and humble structural models such as the shed.

Postmodernism has several characteristic themes, all reactions to the plainness and simplicity of much modernism. It is an architecture that aims to appeal to viewers' minds as well as to their senses in its use of historical references, metaphor (for example, making the facade of a house resemble a face), and deliberate distortions of space to provoke thought. Visually, postmodern architecture is graphic, using curves and arches, strong contrasting colors, and ornament.

Making space complex is a key element in postmodernism, a response to the simple use of space advocated by the "less is more" modernists. Many postmodern architects deliberately call attention to the spaces their buildings surround. For example, a space such as a doorway might be deliberately made smaller or larger than normal, to draw the attention of the visitor passing through. Layering walls in front of walls is another common postmodern method for creating complex spaces. A thin, partitionlike wall punched with cutouts is superimposed over another wall cut with similar openings to create a complicated pattern. The pattern changes as viewers experience it from different angles. Interior space is also broken up into complex patterns by the placement of rooms within larger rooms, among other methods.

Robert Venturi

Robert Venturi is one of the most influential of the postmodern architects. In response to the Bauhaus credo, "Less is more," Venturi came up with his own motto: "Less is a bore." He believed that architecture should take its cue from the complexity and messiness of life itself. This meant that architecture could be hy-

Architect Robert Venturi believed that buildings should be "messy," built using a variety of styles. Venturi greatly admired the effect of the gaudy facades and neon signs of Las Vegas.

materialist resort's roadside architecture as visually powerful and stimulating. Far from criticizing Las Vegas, Venturi praised it as an effective medium to reach its jaded, highway-hypnotized audience of potential consumers. Like the signs and lights of Las Vegas, postmodern architecture could flash its message to society in bold and contemporary language, he argued.

Marvin Trachtenberg and Isabelle Hyman quote Venturi's radical ideas for an architecture for the people:

> He concludes that if we learn our lesson correctly from the strip—and from suburbia—"the archetypal Los Angeles will be our Rome and Las Vegas our Florence; and like the archetypal grain elevators some generations ago, the [Hotel] Flamingo sign will be the model to shock our sensibilities towards a new architecture."[52]

These and other ideas of Venturi's had a revolutionary influence on contemporary architecture.

Robert Venturi's fascination with signs, billboards, and other objects the twentieth-century American encounters daily is clear in his work. He mixes classical architectural elements like columns and arches with such mundane things as used furniture, and symbols from the world of commerce and advertising, like posters and graphics. Another element of his work is exaggeration, as evidenced in the Carll Tucker II House in Katonah, New York (1975). Built with John Rauch and Denise Scott Brown, the house is topped by an oversized pyramid-shaped roof, inset with an enormous round window that dominates the facade. The lower facade contains traditional windows, thus

brid, or made up of several different styles. It also did not have to be deadly serious; it could be sassy and poke fun. It could be repetitive, complex, confusing—anything but impersonal, according to Venturi. The architect also believed in "reopening the door to the past" by honoring history through architecture, something he and other postmodernists felt that the international style, with its emphasis on the future, had neglected.

In 1972 Venturi and his architect wife, Denise Scott Brown, along with another architect, Steven Izenour, published *Learning from Las Vegas*. The book outlines Venturi's philosophy of architecture while taking the reader on a tour of the glitzy desert paradise, with its billboards, garish lights, tacky casinos, and fake Roman statuary. Venturi got readers' attention. They were fascinated with his discussion of the mixing postmodern and traditional styles. Just as the Las Vegas strip can represent a mix of exciting elements—old and new, classic and gaudy—Venturi's architectural view mixes the same elements in an effort to wake up a public grown sleepy from too much machine-age monotony.

Chestnut Hill House

Robert Venturi's Chestnut Hill House in Philadelphia (1962) has been called ugly. It is modeled after a conventional suburban house of wood frame and stucco, with a typical pitched (slanting) roof, two porches, and a central chimney. Again using the startling exaggeration and distortion of reality he admired in Las Vegas architecture, Venturi made sure that the house was anything but typical. Its roof is stretched artificially high. The front of the house is split down the middle by a long vertical gap that slices clear to the enlarged porch, which is little more than a square chunk cut into the facade. The porch is topped with an imitation arch whose only purpose is to decorate the otherwise plain exterior. Chestnut Hill House's unusually large size, cubelike structure, and borrowed historical details (such as the false arch) make a puzzling picture. Confusing an audience was part of Venturi's plan: He believed that architecture should engage people in "dialogue," almost as though he were having a conversation with the viewer through his building designs.

Venturi's Chestnut Hill House uses a classic suburban style and twists it with unusual additions that some deem ugly.

Stern's TV-Headed Woman

Robert Stern is another contemporary architect whose influences were similar to those of Robert Venturi and Charles Moore. In Architecture, *Marvin Trachtenburg and Isabelle Hyman give an amusing example of his work.*

"The particular obsession of the New York architect Robert Stern has been the ancient [column] orders, which he has subjected to transformation saturated with wit, invention, and insight. In his unexecuted project for a storefront for Best Products, Inc. (a catalogue retailer of household goods), Stern's ingenuity is seen at its extreme. . . . In the small side unit [of the facade] [an] image takes over: of a 'fat woman' whose head is formed by the TV-shaped 'metope' [a design element in a Greek temple] above, its hollow core destined for the display of the Best products, inescapably suggesting that the 'idiot box' has taken control of and replaced the consumer's brain. . . . Stern's . . . slur on society-at-large [is] so funny (and so close to the undeniable truth) that no one can really take offense."

Charles Moore

Charles Moore is a contemporary of Robert Venturi and has shared many of his ideas. Like Venturi, he believes that a building should have symbolic meaning and should call upon the ghosts of the past. Moore also had a commitment to what he called "the making of places," according to Trachtenberg and Hyman:

By the 1960s, particularly in America, and most particularly in suburbanized car cultures as found in California, where Moore taught and practiced, places had begun to look disturbingly alike: this street like that, this shopping mall . . . like that one. . . . The result was a . . . disorientation perhaps only intuitively felt by most people, yet nevertheless an increasing ill of contemporary civilization. Moore's aim was to recapture, if only piecemeal and metaphorically, the lost "sense of place."[53]

Thus, Moore used his knowledge of architectural history to bring character and style back into the bland contemporary environment of crackerbox houses that looked all the same.

Kresge College Dormitory Complex

Moore created a unique sense of place with his dormitory complex at Kresge College in Santa Cruz, California (1965–1974). Meant to resemble the main street of a quaint mountain town, the complex's central pathway rambles past dormitories fronted with facades that look like cardboard stage sets. The facades are decorated with a variety of columned screens, stairs, and arches and are accented with bright colors in strategic places, such as the location of a public phone or laundry room, the "monuments" of modern life.

The Piazza d'Italia

Charles Moore created a dramatic, offbeat sense of place with his design for the Piazza d'Italia in New Orleans (1975–1980). The intention of the site was to provide Italian-American residents with a source of ethnic pride and a place to celebrate an annual festival. Moore went all out in drawing on an overwhelming variety of historical buildings in his design, including the Trevi fountain in Rome and the Place des Victoires in Paris. The result is a delightful fantasy blending history and imagination. The piazza is filled with humorous detail, such as the waterspout heads that are sculptures of Charles Moore's own face. The grouping of arches represents a lighthearted tribute to the classical style in which each type of traditional column order is represented. However, instead of placing arches in a

The Piazza d'Italia in New Orleans, designed by Charles Moore, is filled with lighthearted elements that typify postmodern architecture. Moore's experimental and whimsical use of ancient design elements heavily influenced other architects.

A Stage-Set Village

In his book Body, Memory, and Architecture, *coauthored with Kent C. Bloomer, postmodern architect Charles Moore recounts reasons behind his design for the Kresge College dormitory complex at the University of Santa Cruz, as well as his delight in seeing the "village" enjoyed by the students living there.*

"The scheme [for Kresge College] . . . was based on a pedestrian street winding up on the ridge in the forest tightly flanked by buildings, their fronts painted white to bring light into this passage in the dark forest. (The other sides of the buildings, facing the forest, are painted a dark ochre, so as to merge into the trees.) The imagery of whitewalled galleries along a winding street is, of course, of a village, and the intimacy of a village is a useful model. But . . . there is no mayor, no rich or poor. . . . There are, instead, aspects of makebelieve. . . . The choreographic possibilities of such a vision fascinated the architects [Charles Moore and William Turnbull], and they fashioned the white gallery walls, which they painted bright colors on their reverse sides, into cut-out planes, like stage flats, adding other cut-out walls so that people walking in the street, especially conscious of their own bodies moving *through* planes, would feel themselves important, like dancers on a stage. . . . The buildings are carefully and consciously stage sets, for a drama improvised by the inhabitants. An exciting moment for the architects came one Halloween, when at twilight jack-o'-lanterns appeared along the gallery rails and white-sheeted figures wailed ghostly sounds as they danced up the street."

historically accurate grouping, Moore plucked their images out of the past and organized them into a new, refreshing pattern that is very much in the present. Moore even outlined some of the columns in pink neon. The brightly colored, arched and columned monument is saved from mere silliness by its unified and sincere approach.

Charles Moore's flamboyant, energized experimentation with classic forms set the tone for future postmodern architects, including Stanley Tigerman, Michael Graves, and Philip Johnson.

Stanley Tigerman

The whimsical work of Stanley Tigerman, a Chicago architect, demonstrates the postmodern fondness for metaphor, or making buildings stand for other objects. The effect is often playful. Tigerman's Animal Crackers house in Highland Park, Illinois (1978), combines the ordinary wood siding found on many traditional houses with exaggerated, sweeping curves. The front of the house positions two curving windows and a rounded lamp above a doorway in such a way that the windows suggest the mouth, the lamp the snout, of a smiling animal. Tigerman goes all out with visual puns in his design for a two-car garage shaped like the outline of car, and in his House with a Pompadour in Ogne Dunes, Indiana, which was inspired by the owner's hairstyle.

Michael Graves

According to Trachtenberg and Hyman, "No other contemporary architect has penetrated as deeply as has Graves into the Classic form language of both the [arch and post-and-beam] modes, or created with them such powerful and mysterious new images."[54]

One of Michael Graves's most important buildings is the Portland Public Service Building (1980–1983). The Portland building's cubelike structure resembles a child's tower of blocks—not surprisingly, since Graves has said that he likes to de-

Architect Michael Graves won many design awards for his Portland Public Service building. Graves, who says he likes to design buildings as a child would, uses Peg-Board and block-like forms.

sign buildings as though he were a child. The building's bright colors are also child-like. Small windows dot the cream-colored facade, making it resemble a Peg-Board. One side of the cube takes the form of a huge mirrored window, while the other side is decorated with pillars that some viewers feel resemble either a face or a giant man's figure standing guard against the building. The pillars can also be taken as a reference to classical architecture, rising toward the wedge shape that can be seen as a giant keystone (the triangular stone at the top of a classical arch).

The Portland Public Service Building was the first public building commissioned in the postmodern style, and many Portlanders disliked it. The seagreen tiles decorating its base were even compared to bathroom tiles by some contemptuous viewers. Its nontraditional colors, shapes, and patterns unnerved people in the late twentieth century, just as the Eiffel Tower had unnerved people a hundred years before. However, the building was respected by architects. The American Institute of Architecture awarded it one of its eleven honor awards for 1983.

Philip Johnson

Philip Johnson is an important figure in contemporary architecture. His work has been sought after by big corporations eager to advertise themselves through their buildings. Johnson was reportedly paid more than $200 million by AT&T to design their new headquarters in New York (1978). The 647-foot-high tower is a delightful switch from the glass-box skyscrapers of the sixties. The building's top is cut

Architect Philip Johnson designed the AT&T headquarters in New York City to resemble a huge piece of furniture. Many postmodern architects use similar touches of humor in their designs.

with a half-moon scroll that makes it clearly resemble a piece of furniture. It has often been compared to a gigantic highboy or dresser. The top could also be meant to represent a pay phone coin slot, with the building's entrance standing for the coin return slot. The humor of the structure does not subtract from its beauty.

The postmodernists' startling and complicated use of space is spectacularly dramatized in a Parisian building, the Centre Pompidou (1977). Designed by Richard Rogers and Renzo Piano, the

The Centre Pompidou in Paris houses an art museum, a library, and an industrial design center. With its exposed beams and pipes, the center looks like a work in progress rather than a finished design.

building houses an art museum, a library, and an industrial design center. However, what is outside the building is quite surprising. All the pipes, tubes, ducts, and other structural elements that are usually hidden are plainly visible on the outside walls. The building's exposed inner workings are painted in primary colors. The Centre Pompidou looks like a project still under construction, or else turned inside out. On the west wall, nearly all glass, a large glass tube containing an escalator zigzags from ground level to a rooftop restaurant. The Centre Pompidou is one of the most unusual and controversial buildings of the twentieth century, and it makes imaginative use of many of the ideas of postmodernism.

Future Directions

Thus, the twentieth century has swung full circle from the international style's no-frills approach, to the the wild extrava-

gance and irreverence of contemporary practitioners. Where will architecture go from here?

In part, the shape of tomorrow's buildings will depend on what the people of tomorrow are like. Political, economic, and social factors will affect building styles, just as they have influenced them in the past.

Writer Anita Abramovitz points out that as our technology continues to make warp-speed advances in efficiency, we will be forced to make choices about our architectural needs. For example, advanced engineering has already eliminated the physical need for windows in a building, since interior climates can be controlled. We may choose to keep windows as mere decorative trimming. Or we may find other practical uses for them—as solar heat sources, for example.

Our feelings about each other will influence how we build. Will we want to live in open communities or behind high-tech fortresses to protect ourselves from crime? If society leans toward buildings with heavy security, which is the current trend in gated communities and security-patrolled office buildings, this emphasis on crime prevention will influence our buildings' appearance and comfort level. Structural elements that could be affected include lighting, the number and placement of exits, and many other factors.

Humans have experienced an explosion of technological progress in all areas. Architecture has kept pace with other developments, as a glance at the skyline of any prosperous city reveals. Tall buildings are everywhere. The postmodern style's reaction against skyscrapers did not prevent contemporary architecture from producing more towering structures than ever before. As Abramovitz points out, some people applaud the human progress that skyscrapers symbolize, while other disapprove of the huge buildings that threaten to block out the sky.

For good or bad, skyscrapers have changed the world's urban areas. Cities are still contending with the traffic congestion brought on by increased commuting to downtown office buildings, and once-thriving downtown neighborhoods are gone for good, torn down or turned into urban ghettos. On the other hand, many of the open areas beneath skyscrapers have been transformed into attractive shopping malls, pedestrian arcades, and other urban havens. It will be up to the people of the twenty-first century to continue to deal with the consequences of high-rise buildings as the trend continues.

The postmodernists refocused attention on the importance of history. Future generations will need to decide how important it is to preserve our architectural heritage. Will classic buildings be torn down to make way for new ones? Or will people decide to spend the money neces-

The World Trade Center in New York City typifies the modern skyscraper. From ancient to modern times, the desire to build memorable structures that awe and mystify people remains a goal of architects.

sary to restore them? Improved technology will no doubt suggest improved methods of restoring old structures and protecting new ones from damage by fire and flood, earthquake and hurricane.

Whatever the future holds, people will always build, not only for shelter, but to satisfy their longing for beauty. As our knowledge of the environment and our place in it continues to grow, our definition of architecture will grow also. Someday, thanks to a truly progressive architecture, we may find ourselves living in harmony with one another and with our natural surroundings in a way that satisfies our spirits.

Notes

Chapter 1: The Ancient World

1. Helen Leacroft and Richard Leacroft, *The Buildings of Ancient Egypt*. New York: William R. Scott, 1963.
2. Leacroft and Leacroft, *The Buildings of Ancient Egypt*.
3. Marvin Trachtenberg and Isabelle Hyman, *Architecture: From Prehistory to Post-Modernism*. New York: Harry N. Abrams, 1986.
4. Victoria Kloss Ball, *Architecture and Interior Design: A Basic History Through the Seventeenth Century*. New York: Wiley, 1980.
5. Trachtenberg and Hyman, *Architecture*.
6. Leacroft and Leacroft, *The Buildings of Ancient Egypt*.
7. Ball, *Architecture and Interior Design*.
8. Trachtenberg and Hyman, *Architecture*.
9. Ball, *Architecture and Interior Design*.
10. Susan Woodford, *The Parthenon*. Minneapolis: Lerner, 1981.
11. Woodford, *The Parthenon*.
12. Ball, *Architecture and Interior Design*.
13. Trachtenberg and Hyman, *Architecture*.
14. Ball, *Architecture and Interior Design*.
15. Ball, *Architecture and Interior Design*.

Chapter 2: The Middle Ages

16. Anita Abramovitz, *People and Spaces: A View of History Through Architecture*. New York: Viking, 1979.
17. Ball, *Architecture and Interior Design*.
18. Trachtenberg and Hyman, *Architecture*.
19. Trachtenberg and Hyman, *Architecture*.
20. Ball, *Architecture and Interior Design*.
21. Trachtenberg and Hyman, *Architecture*.
22. Ball, *Architecture and Interior Design*.
23. Trachtenberg and Hyman, *Architecture*.
24. Trachtenberg and Hyman, *Architecture*.

Chapter 3: Islam's Influence and Gothic Architecture

25. Trachtenberg and Hyman, *Architecture*.

26. Trachtenberg and Hyman, *Architecture*.
27. George Sullivan, *Understanding Architecture*. New York: Frederick Warne, 1971.
28. Abramovitz, *People and Spaces*.
29. Ball, *Architecture and Interior Design*.
30. Quoted in Sullivan, *Understanding Architecture*.

Chapter 4: Renaissance and Baroque Architecture

31. Ball, *Architecture and Interior Design*.
32. Trachtenberg and Hyman, *Architecture*.
33. Ball, *Architecture and Interior Design*.
34. Trachtenberg and Hyman, *Architecture*.
35. Trachtenberg and Hyman, *Architecture*.
36. Sullivan, *Understanding Architecture*.
37. Abramovitz, *People and Spaces*.
38. Sullivan, *Understanding Architecture*.
39. Trachtenberg and Hyman, *Architecture*.
40. Ball, *Architecture and Interior Design*.

Chapter 5: The Eighteenth and Nineteenth Centuries

41. *Thomas Jefferson's University*. Charlottesville, VA: Thomasson-Grant, 1987.
42. *Thomas Jefferson's University*.
43. Trachtenberg and Hyman, *Architecture*.
44. Abramovitz, *People and Spaces*.
45. Trachtenberg and Hyman, *Architecture*.

Chapter 6: Modern Architecture

46. James Cross Giblin, *The Skyscraper Book*. New York: Crowell, 1981.
47. Sullivan, *Understanding Architecture*.
48. Giblin, *The Skyscraper Book*.
49. Giblin, *The Skyscraper Book*.
50. Giblin, *The Skyscraper Book*.
51. Trachtenberg and Hyman, *Architecture*.

Chapter 7: Contemporary Architecture

52. Trachtenberg and Hyman, *Architecture*.
53. Trachtenberg and Hyman, *Architecture*.
54. Trachtenberg and Hyman, *Architecture*.

Glossary

arcade: A row of arches supported on columns.

arcuate construction: A building system of arches, vaults, and domes.

barrel vault (also called a tunnel vault): An arch that extends lengthwise and becomes a tunnel-like roof.

basilica: A Roman public building converted by early Christians into churches.

buttress: A projecting mass that keeps an exterior wall from collapsing outward.

cantilever: A projecting beam supported at one end.

capital: The top of a column.

cella: A room inside a Greek or Roman temple, usually containing a statue of a god or goddess.

Corinthian: A type of Greek column with a capital representing a cluster of acanthus leaves.

dome: A circular vault or roof made up of arches radiating around a common center.

Doric: A style of Greek column, thicker than the Ionic column, with a cushion-like capital.

facade: The front wall of a building.

flute: A vertical groove in a Greek or Roman column.

groin vault: A cross-shaped roof vault consisting of two barrel vaults at right angles.

Ionic: A type of Greek column, thinner than the Doric column, with a scrolled capital.

megalithic construction: A building system of stacked stones, assembled without mortar.

minaret: A slender balconied tower; part of a mosque.

mosque: An Islamic house of worship.

nave: A rectangular open space in a church.

pendentives: Curving stone triangles that fill in the spaces between a dome and its supporting noncircular stonework.

pinnacle: A small tower with a pointed roof, usually found on top of a buttress on a Gothic cathedral.

post-and-beam construction (also called post-and-lintel): A building system of vertical pillars spanned by horizontal beams.

pylon: The massive stone gate on an Egyptian temple.

rib vaults: Skeletal arches that support roof vaulting.

transept: A high open area crossing a church's nave at right angles.

vault: A rounded ceiling or roof made from a series of arches.

For Further Reading

Anita Abramovitz, *People and Spaces: A View of History Through Architecture*. New York: Viking, 1979. A well-written and thought-provoking discussion that places architecture in a social and historical framework. Covers the full range of history from prehistoric architecture through contemporary architecture. Projects are not covered in detail.

James Cross Giblin, *The Skyscraper Book*. New York: Crowell, 1981. An enjoyable and thorough account of the history of the skyscraper, containing interesting technical and historical detail. Looks at each project individually.

David Jacobs, *Master Builders of the Middle Ages*. New York: American Heritage, 1969. An interesting and readable survey of the architecture of the Middle Ages; heavily illustrated. Discusses history leading up to the time period and tells how religion and custom influenced architecture.

Helen Leacroft and Richard Leacroft, *The Buildings of Ancient Egypt*. New York: William R. Scott, 1963. A simple, easy-to-follow discussion of ancient Egypt and its architecture: The social life and customs of the people are explained.

———, *The Buildings of Ancient Mesopotamia*. New York: Young-Scott, 1974. Simple discussion of the architecture and customs of ancient Mesopotamia.

George Sullivan, *Understanding Architecture*. New York: Frederick Warne, 1971. A miniature survey of all the important architectural movements. Clear, accurate, and easy to follow, this book is an excellent source for information on architecture's history and technical advances. Discusses individual projects in detail.

Thomas Jefferson's University. Charlottesville, VA: Thomasson-Grant,1987. A beautifully illustrated pamphlet discussing in detail the University of Virginia campus designed by Thomas Jefferson. Contains historical quotes.

Susan Woodford, *The Parthenon*. Minneapolis: Lerner, 1981. Well-written, thoughtful, detailed account of one of architecture's most influential and well-known buildings. Contains sections on the way the Parthenon was built and on the customs of the Romans.

Additional Works Consulted

Victoria Kloss Ball, *Architecture and Interior Design: A Basic History Through the Seventeenth Century.* New York: Wiley, 1980. A thoughtful and interesting discussion, but the author's style and vocabulary make it difficult reading at times. Also discusses interior design for each time period through the seventeenth century.

George Barford, *Understanding Modern Architecture.* Worcester, MA: Davis, 1986. A very readable and thorough discussion of modern architecture. Includes an introductory overview of architecture in general, discussing stylistic periods and history. Contains information on many lesser-known modern and postmodern architects.

Kent C. Bloomer and Charles Moore, *Body, Memory, and Architecture.* New Haven, CT: Yale University Press, 1977. A complex philosophical look at postmodern architecture. Charles Moore is one of the best-known postmodern architects.

Jacob Bronowski, *The Ascent of Man.* Boston: Little, Brown, 1973. A fascinating, readable, humanistic discussion of human history. While not about architecture alone, it examines architecture in some detail. Discusses the post-and-beam and arch building systems, as well as ancient Cretan and Islamic architecture.

Christian Norberg-Schulz, *Baroque Architecture.* New York: Harry N. Abrams, 1971. A thorough treatment of the architecture and history of the period, heavily illustrated. Difficult vocabulary.

Marvin Trachtenberg and Isabelle Hyman, *Architecture: From Prehistory to Post-Modernism.* New York: Harry N. Abrams, 1986. A complete and fascinating reference book covering the history of architecture up through the 1980s. Often the descriptions of individual architectural projects use complex vocabulary. Contains helpful historical summaries that place the discussions in context. Excellent photographs and illustrations.

Frank Lloyd Wright, *Testament.* New York: Horizon Press, 1957. Wright's views on architecture and life in general in his own poetic commentary. Shifts from topic to topic, thus a little hard to follow. Difficult vocabulary. Includes extensive illustrations.

Index

Credits

Cover photo by Archiv für Kunst und Geschichte, Berlin

Alinari/Art Resource, NY, 15, 21 (both), 26, 27, 29, 36 (bottom), 39, 50 (top), 51, 52, 54, 55, 56, 60

Architectural Association, 63, 73

Art Resource, NY, 49, 68, 88 (bottom)

The Bettmann Archive, 50 (bottom), 65 (bottom), 74 (right), 79, 80, 81, 89, 90 (top)

© Tom Clark/Architectural Association, 98

Ted Feder/Art Resource, NY, 66

Foto Marburg/Art Resource, NY, 33, 42, 91

French Government Tourist Office, 69, 76

© Taylor Galyean/Architectural Association, 96

Giraudon/Art Resource, NY, 31, 41, 47, 90 (bottom)

© Bernard Godfrey, Architectural Association, 100

© Andrew Higgott, Architectural Association, 88 (top)

© E. R. Jarrett/ Architectural Association, 65 (top)

© Joe Kerr/Architectural Association, 99

Erich Lessing/Art Resource, NY, 45

© A. Minchin/Architectural Association, 87, 94

North Wind Picture Archives, 14, 19, 22 (both), 23

© C. Parson/Architectural Association, 62

Reuters/Bettmann, 85

Scala/Art Resource, NY, 35, 36 (top)

SEF/Art Resource, NY, 58

© Graeme Shankland/Architectural Association, 64

UPI/Bettmann, 12, 74 (left), 82, 86, 93, 101

Vanni/Art Resource, NY, 11, 30, 70, 71 (both)

Grateful acknowledgment is made to the following for permission to reproduce portions of their material: From *Architecture: From Prehistory to Post-Modernism* by Marvin Trachtenberg and Isabelle Hyman. Published in 1986 by Harry N. Abrams, Inc., New York. All rights reserved.

About the Author

Paula Bryant Pratt is a writer and copy editor who lives in California. Her writing credits for Lucent Books include *The Importance of Martha Graham* and *Maps: Plotting Places on the Globe*. Pratt holds a master's degree in American literature. She and her husband Michael, a computer programmer, have a two-year-old daughter, Cerise Olivia.